Dark Psychology

Why YOU NEED to Learn NOW secrets techniques to influence people with Manipulation, Persuasion, Deception, Mind Control, Covert NLP and Brainwashing + BONUS (How to use dark psychology in daily life)

By Jason Goleman

Table of Contents

Introduction

Welcome to Dark Psychology: The Ultimate Beginner's Guide to Persuasion, Manipulation, Deception, Mind Control & How They Are Used to Influence People! Thank you for downloading our unbeatable guide on Dark Psychology and the different methods and techniques involved in learning to master it for your own personal benefit or becoming more informed in order to protect yourself and others from the darker side of the human mind.

Psychology is the study of how humans think, feel and react to different situations based on the emotional, physical and mental elements that play a role in determining an individual's behavior. Dark Psychology covers all of those factors and elements that are often difficult to discuss with other people, uncomfortable to admit that we need assistance with managing (sometimes professionally or medically) and even deny exist because they are too malicious or frightening to acknowledge.

The following chapters will discuss topics related to Dark Psychology and influencing people such as:

- The art of persuasion and the different types of techniques that includes like Covert Persuasion and Dark Persuasion tactics
- The wide range of psychological methods that are at work in the world each day and how to spot them
- Professional tips and tricks related to the understanding and mastering of Dark Psychology from experts around the world
- Relatable examples of psychologically manipulative and influential techniques in real world situations
- How to identify predatory behavior and see through the walls and masks people hide behind when they want people to see them in a certain light

Have you ever wanted to know how people get others to hang on their every word and follow their every suggestion? Have you wondered how cults that seem so dangerous and threatening when being observed from the outside manage to draw in people to make their beliefs and their secluded community stronger? The use of psychological techniques such as persuasion, manipulation, and brainwashing is just a small part of how these types of predators and Master Manipulators gain control over others and use them to forward their own goals and lifestyle enhancement.

There is an overwhelming amount of information available to the point that it can feel impossible to find your way through Dark Psychology and all of the various areas of study included in the field. The best way to move forward is to feed your curiosity on the topic and seek out all of the facts, practical steps and exercises you can find! Downloading our guide was a great place to start and we hope that you find everything you want to know within the following chapters.

Thanks again for choosing *Dark Psychology: The Ultimate Beginner's Guide To Persuasion, Manipulation, Deception, Mind Control & How They Are Used To Influence People*! Every effort has been made to ensure it is full of as much useful and practical information that is available on the subject, regardless of your personal reasons for taking an interest. Please enjoy the guide and congratulations on starting your journey through the dark side of psychology!

Chapter 1: Getting Better Acquainted With The Concept Of Dark Psychology

Understanding why people are the way that we are has been a topic of emotional, philosophical, behavioral and psychological study in one form or another since human beings became self-aware through evolution. Our ability to comprehend, to imagine and to change the way ourselves and others view the world through slight alterations in thinking or seeing are just some of the amazing talents that the human brain is capable of. With all the good aspects of life that are boosted by and all of the inventions developed from the human mind, many people hesitate to think about the shadowy side of human thought, emotion, and behavior and how it stems from the wondrous mental organ that keeps the rest of the body running as it should.

Despite those who would rather not think about the darker side of humanity, there are those in the world of psychology that have dedicated their lives to:

- Identifying characteristics and emotional traits
- Monitoring and studying individual behaviors

- Understanding points of view and definitions of the world
- Predicting dangerous or harmful behaviors individuals may be capable of doing to themselves or others
- Using the information gathered over decades of study to better understand dark personality types and create profiles based on past behaviors in an attempt to get a better overall understanding of the criminal mind

Some of the most well-known and respected uses for psychology in human society include:

- Building better teams in work, sports, research teams or any other discipline where people need to rely on each other in order to achieve a goal
- Building stronger relationships with friends and family thanks to a greater understanding of emotional responses
- Improved diplomatic relations between countries through enhanced communication and negotiation skills
- Increasing productivity in offices or other professional settings
- Mental health understanding and improvement
- Treatment of emotional and psychological conditions

There are as many reasons for being interested in Dark Psychology as there are areas to study within the subject. It all comes down to how you choose to use it or protect yourself from it as soon as you know about the type of people, circumstances, situations, statements, and actions to keep an eye out for. We'll be starting our journey through the darker side of the human mind by taking a closer look at the concept of Dark Psychology, its history and the different elements that make it one of the most fascinating topics related to the brain and how it works on the most primal and private levels.

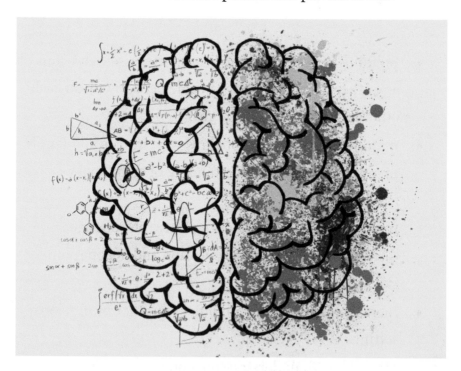

<u>What Is Dark Psychology?</u>

The topic of psychology is one that captures the attention of millions around the world and has become invaluable in matters of both health and justice. Unfortunately, psychology also has a negative cloud around it that makes people hesitate before trusting their own psychological health and concerns to the expertise of others. In most cases, this hesitation comes from lack of familiarity or understanding with what psychology is and how can be used daily to improve people's daily lives. The study of psychology has made a massive impact on human self-awareness and understanding of emotions, but the topic as a whole reaches far greater and makes a much greater impact on our daily lives than many give it credit for.

Psychology is defined as the study of the science behind the thoughts, emotions and actions that govern each human based on their own personal history or inclination toward learned or developed behaviors. In other words, people who study psychology are driven by curiosity and quest for knowledge about why people are the way that we are. Dark Psychology takes that study into the hidden parts of the human mind, the areas that people try to ignore, to bury or to cover (if they are even aware of them). Others use their familiarity with dark psychological techniques in order to influence the thoughts of others, gain control over others or manipulate people into doing what they're told, sometimes without ever suspecting their thoughts or actions weren't their own. Some of the most commonly read about and discussed sub-sections of Dark Psychology include:

- Cyberstalking and other virtual predatory behavior
  - This category also includes personalities as mild as internet trolls on social media sites to the most severe like virtual identity thieves
- Political psychology falls into the realm of Dark Psychology, depending on who the subject of study is
- Behavioral psychology majors spend a fair amount of time studying the traits of Dark Psychology and how they can influence the behavior of different types of people
- There are a number of Dark Psychology techniques at use and in practice with those use the art of self-promotion to enhance their careers. Those who have made lasting marks of the entertainment industry and those who dominate many artistic careers have thanked psychological tactics of persuasion and reading people for furthering their success in their chosen fields.

Each person's experience with Dark Psychology in their personal life all depends on an individual's personality and if they're the type to try to keep themselves from being the victims of dark psychological techniques or if they're the type to use them on others as a way of advancing their own position, benefiting from a certain situation or knowingly causing harm.

Looking Back Into the History of Dark Psychology & Its Impact on the Modern World

If Dark Psychology is such a topic of interest, why is it still considered such a new and hardly established branch of the psychological world? One of the main reasons for that is because while psychology as a whole is still a newer concept where the history of medicine is concerned, Dark Psychology as a field of study is one of the newest developments within psychology since its acceptance into mainstream society as a serious subject.

Dark Psychology made its mark on the field in the early 2000s when psychologists all over the world became determined and driven to better understand cybercriminals began gathering knowledge that had been collected on criminal psychology and profiling people in order to help catch them or predict their next attacks before they ever got a chance to set them off. Research into the individual traits associated with Dark Psychology (also known as the traits of malevolence) has gone on for decades, leading to some of the greatest developments injustice and criminal law across the globe such as:

- Criminal profiling and investigative branches of service dedicated to its study and enhancement at levels of government from county level cops to international investigative units
- New laws put in place protecting people from the most malicious among us that may not have been able to be dealt with by law before
- Extending punishment sentences for the most malevolent or getting them medical and psychological treatment for their conditions that were not recognized by medical or legal circles in the years before a particular event

Today, Dark Psychology is of best known as being of particular interest to those studying the minds, thoughts, and actions of criminals that work within the virtual realm for practical use and global benefit. There have been countless uses made for it in the entertainment business that continues to be explored including high quality and informative shows on real crimes cases to fictional criminals and crime solvers with depth and humanizing qualities that have caught the attention of people in all finance, professional, social and class levels around the world.

More than anything else, Dark Psychology and its growing popularity have forced even those in the most denial about the darker side of human nature to stand up and take notice, accepting that there is the possibility of darker traits making themselves known in even the happiest and optimistic of people. Each person is made of up both positive and negative traits, characteristics and behaviors that are inspired or designed by the events we survive and the people we surround ourselves with. It's perfectly natural for each person to have questions about their nature, their thoughts, their emotions and actions that can be answered by the research and studies being done in the area of Dark Psychology.

The Effects Of Dark Psychology On Human Beings

There are nine personality traits that psychologists most commonly identify with those who do well with Dark Psychology for personal use or as a subject of study throughout their personal and private lives. Sometimes known as the Traits of Malevolence, these character markers make up the foundations of darker personalities and understanding them can help with identifying their use around you, intentional or unknown.

Pro Tip: It Takes At Least Two To Make A Pattern

Having just one of the traits identifiable is not enough for someone to solidly be labeled a dark personality. If they only fall into one category of markers, then it could just be a chance development from some youthful trauma or difficult set of circumstances they survived that turned out to have a major influence on the creation of that individual's personality. In cases like these where the trait is harmful to the person or to others, or where the individual is unable to accept this part of themselves and it leads to other psychological difficulties, the person should seek the help of a psychologist or other psychological health care professional to identify their concerns and figure out together how best to treat them moving forward.

Here is a closer look at those characteristics displayed by and identified in people with darker personalities who are driven by their own Dark Psychology.

1. **Narcissism:** Narcissists are individual's whose actions, thoughts and concerns revolve around their own well-being and advancement before others, sometimes at the expense

of others. This character trait is inspired by the Greek myth of Narcissus, a man who wasted his life in love with his own reflection. Narcissists have a tendency to not work well in groups and can be easily offended if others try to supervise them.

2. **Overly Sensitive Egos:** Also commonly referred to as Egotists, people with overly sensitive egos can look similar to Narcissists on paper, but there is a key difference between the two. Like Narcissists, people with overly sensitive egos are most focused on their own advancement and improvement in life, but unlike Narcissists who have a naturally high opinion of themselves, Egotists and others who show this characteristic determine their self-worthy based on what others think of them. When others compliment them, their self-worth increases and they can function without attracting too much attention in their surroundings, whether that is at work or at home. It's when Egotists and those with overly sensitive egos get reprimanded or criticized that their darker nature comes out and it can manifest is a number of ways, as lethargy or anti-social behaviors.

3. **Inflated Self-Interest:** People with inflated self-interests are also focused on their own promotion and well-being, to the point of walking over or abandoning others. This characteristic is often partnered with notable personal ambition and drive that makes them stand out amongst

their peers. Unfortunately, like Narcissists and people with overly sensitive egos, they do not do well in team or group environments but tend to excel in leadership roles and supervising others as long as they have someone to answer to that has a more neutral or balanced personality and behavioral pattern.

4. **Personal Entitlement:** People who are generally and personally entitled believe that they are owed things in this world. While the specifics vary from individual to individual, people who are entitled feel that they deserve what they see others have. It could be superficial like possessions or the amount of money another person makes. It could be deeper like feeling that they deserve love and respect without having to earn it or search for it as most people do. Their darker natures come out when they feel they have been denied something that in their opinion they're entitled to.

   - One of the most common examples of personal entitlement that is used in researching the trait is that of spoiled children. Entitlement is a learned trait that many people grow out of in their teenage years or as they come into adulthood, but it can be encouraged or provoked by elements such as financial standing, social class and personal success (or failure, depending on the individual circumstances).

5. **Manipulative Tendencies:** People who dwell on the dark side of psychology are known for having a talent for manipulation. This may be as mild as using a gift for manipulation to make sure they have the best sales numbers each week to those who use their skills for political advancement and find themselves leading others through thought manipulation and other dangerous techniques.

   - Often called the Machiavellian trait, those who show proficiency for psychological manipulation of others for their own gain are named after the political theorist Niccolò Machiavelli. Machiavelli's political beliefs were based around the idea that the means used to attain a certain goal are always worth the means (often regardless of the cost or damage done, as long as it doesn't negatively affect the individual in question).

6. **Moral Disengagement:** This is the phrase commonly used to describe those who have a way of looking at the world and how it is governed and genuinely believes that the rules in place do not apply to them. People who possess this personality trait are known for thinking they are above the rules and are therefore able to say things or take actions that others would consider unethical or wrong without feeling any kind of moral responsibility, guilt or shame after the fact.

7. **Psychopathy & Psychopathic Tendencies:** Someone who is has been a labeled a psychopath has been identified by professional psychologists or personality experts as having a personality disorder called psychopathy, in which an individual is lacking in empathy or remorse for anyone or anything. The word "psychopath" has entered the common tongue as a well-known descriptive word for serial killers and other criminals that fall into that character type. They've been made famous in television series and horror movies, but this is one of the more misunderstood traits that is still being defined and studied as more and more is discovered about the psychopathic mind.

8. **Sadism & Sadistic Behaviors:** A sadist is someone who has been identified as showing sadistic patterns of behavior or show as part of their formed personality a habit of causing pain or humiliation to others (and gaining pleasure from these actions) as a way of asserting their power and authority over others. The harm does not always have to be physical or psychological. This personality trait is often connected to sexual domination as well as emotional and psychological power assertion.

9. **Spitefulness & Malicious Predispositions:** Malice is the knowing and willingness to cause harm or do evil and spite is the willingness to take this action or this harm even if it means harming themselves in the process (physically,

emotionally or psychologically). These malicious dispositions can manifest in any number of individual characteristics but should be taken very seriously when encountered and handled with the greatest care because the risk of personal damage through interaction is high with those who have regular contact with malicious persons.

The Top Three Traits: The Dark Triad & The Role It Plays In Dark Psychology

While all of the traits listed above are able to be found in people with dark personality types, there are three main elements that some experts argue must be present in order for someone to be considered a subject of Dark Psychology. Manipulation, psychopathy and narcissism form the base elements of what's known in psychological circles as the Dark Triad. The Dark Triad makes the foundation for most Dark Psychology study as the trilogy of traits are the three most common characteristics displayed by those who excel within the realm of Dark Psychology.

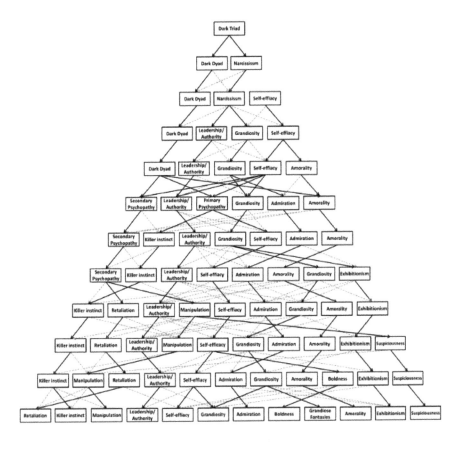

Throughout the course of this guide, we will be taking a more detailed look at the different ways these traits can specifically manifest in different personality types, how to identify their methods and how to protect yourself from them. Keep reading to learn more about the dark side of human psychology and how it is at work just about everywhere you look from popular advertising campaigns to people you pass in the street!

Chapter 2: Who Uses Dark Psychology To Influence People?

How To Identify A Predator Before Becoming A Victim

When people hear the word "predator", many automatically think of panthers stalking smaller animals through the trees or picture rows of razor-sharp teeth from a meat-eating dinosaur painting from their childhood museum trip memories. While it is true that the term is usually reserved for animals that are known for hunting, the actual definition of a predator covers more than animal instinct. Predators are defined as beings that naturally prey on or exploit others for their own benefit. In the case of animals, this is basically the definition of the Circle of Life or the natural order of things. It is understandable that in order to survive, some species feed on other species. This concept only becomes unsettling when survival is taken out of the equation, and the animal in question (in the case of Dark Psychology and its studies, a human being) is preying on and exploiting others for the pleasure of it or out of gluttony.

A noticeable skill set for the art of deception is a common trait amongst predators, the details of which we will cover more thoroughly throughout this chapter. Of all the personality types identified in the research of Dark Psychology, the predator is one of the most commonly found and the most dangerous if left unmonitored. Get to know the predatory type, some of their most effective tricks for daily use and how to protect yourself from them when they wheedle their way into surroundings (or even into your trust).

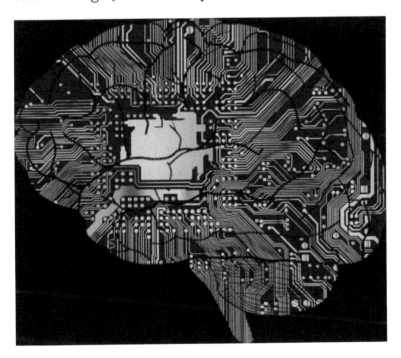

What Is A Human Predator?

As logical and self-aware human beings, most people understand and can see the difference in that taking prey for survival is the way of the world, but that taking advantage of more vulnerable people or creatures when life isn't on the line is wrong. Predators (regardless of what sub-section of categorization they fall into) cannot make this distinction and are not concerned by the fact that they do not comprehend this as the average person does.

A Human Predator is someone who uses their understanding of human desires, thought manipulation, and the general mental state of every person they meet to always know how to control and take advantage of them when the time comes. Human Predators do not make connections with other people unless there is some way to benefit from that relationship, either by achieving a certain goal or by acquiring something they want or need. There are a range of different types of Human Predators that have been identified, but there are countless studies being performed around the world that are endeavoring to narrow the definitions of predator groups in order to gain a better understanding of how to treat or handle them if treatment is not an option. Experts also study human nature and new findings that are printed each in search of identifying and defining other potential predatory personalities, actions or behaviors that could be used to prevent or capture predators before they can cause irreversible harm to themselves and others.

There are an endless number of circumstances that can cause an emotional reaction in humans. Using years of study in psychology and the more specific fields such as Dark Psychology, experts have dedicated their lives and careers to answering the question of whether or not it is possible to predict how people will react. The following chart shows a list of common human behaviors on the left and the most commonly reported reactions in areas of both live testing and widespread mental health surveys. While this may not always be the case (individual circumstances, a person's psychological state and general attitude all have a bearing on emotional reactions), these have shown to be the most documented and understood among psychologists around the world.

Problem	Emotion
Being alone at night	Fear of being stalked by a predator
Sexual infidelity	Sexual jealousy
Social ridicule	Social anxiety
Uneven reciprocity exchanges	Pride, humiliation, obligation
Being cheated	Anger
Considering cheating or not fulfilling an expectation	Anxiety
Having cheated others	Guilt
Another individual has an unjustified favorable status	Envy

Different Types Of Human Predators & How To Spot Them

Human Predators are people who have no issue (morally, emotionally or psychologically) with making life difficult for others, especially when the results of the action make life easier for themselves in the process. Not every predator has the same motive, drive, goal or method so it is important to know how some of the more prevalent types of Human

Predators and how to identify them so that you are ready no matter when or where you encounter these people.

- **Social Predator:** A Social Predator is someone who is driven by a desire to overcome every obstacle and sees everything from a friendly game of catch to a company sporting event as a critical competitive hurdle for them to conquer. Their need to win at everything makes socializing difficult for them and their inflated egos are easily bruised, particularly if questioned in front of their peers or people they see as inferior.
  - One of the most frequently exhibited personality traits of Social Predators is their base desire to win at everything. This could be in serious matters such as establishing dominance in a room full of co-workers or it could be in simple conversations such as small talk in an elevator. They are interested in their own advancement in both personal and professional matters and see their route to their goals as being achieved by improving their social standing or making important connections that could be relied upon in times of struggle.
  - Most people meet Social Predators in the workplace, becoming the victim of their verbal and mental abuse at the office. While their

determination and eye for details make people who classify as Social Predators potentially efficient and productive employees, they do not work well with others, making team projects or events impossibilities without considerable negotiation or behavioral monitoring from someone they acknowledge as superior.

- While it is less common, Social Predators can display violent attitude changes and physically abusive behavior in their personal, private and romantic encounters.

- **Sexual Predator:** A Sexual Predator is someone who gains control over another person or their thoughts and actions through sexual conquest, often by physically, mentally or psychologically malevolent means. The term "Sexual Predator" is most often associated with adults who target children, earn their trust and then prey on their immaturity and lack of worldly experience to take advantage of them for personal gain or satisfaction.

  - Predators get their name from their animalistic or primal behaviorisms and ways of viewing their fellow human beings. One identifiable characteristic that is associated with predators is how they choose their prey or hunting grounds. Social Predators for example are able to use their carefully developed social skills to work their techniques in almost any settings. Sexual Predators on the other hand are better able to put their specializations into action in familiar and controlled settings, targeting a specific type of person or chain of events.

- The term first came to use in the mainstream culture in the mid-1980s and is typically saved for those who not only are known to hunt like predators through sexual means but have also been recorded as committing a sexually violent act in the past.

- **Virtual, Cyber or Online Predator:** This category of predators refers to those people who take advantage of others for their own gain through the use of technology and technological advancements like social media, online chat groups, dating apps, community board sites, and a seemingly endless list of virtual scams.

  - Identity theft is one of the most commonly discussed virtual crimes committed by Cyber Predators. The process of proving it can be grueling and it can take years to recover from financially and where credit is concerned.

  - This is one of the predatory behavioral types that those fascinated in studying Dark Psychology choose a topic of research or detailed interest. Cyber Predators are a growing concern as more and more of our daily lives become digital or virtual from getting paid to save money for retirement, communicating securely with friends and family to sharing delicate information in critical situations without fear of it being stolen, intercepted or copied.

- Due to the fact that all communication with Cyber Predators is done virtually, it can be nearly impossible to locate these criminals and dangerous individuals or groups that use the internet as a limitless hunting ground. Many of the new advancements in cybersecurity designed to protect the vulnerable or unfamiliar with virtual interactions can also be used to shelter and protect those who are using the virtual world for nefarious means.

- **Emotional Predator:** This type of predator is often lumped in with general predators who are still being processed for a more specific categorization. They are defined as people who feel positive and pleasured by causing harm to others. What specifically separates Emotional Predators from a general classification of those with predatory behavior is that their typical hunting ground involves victims that are targeted for their romantic relationship potential. Emotional Predators build romantic relationships not out of a desire for companionship but in order to benefit in some way whether it is from focused emotional and psychological harm over time as the relationship grows or the benefit could also be financial, with the predator forming a relationship in order to divorce their spouse later for monetary gain.

There are a variety of other predatory labels that people can be given, depending on their behaviors and their ultimate motive for the techniques they perfect through practice or the people they target in their favored hunting grounds. The best way to protect yourself and the people you love from predators is not to memorize all the different types, but rather to understand the general markers that can be used to identify someone showing off predatory thoughts and actions.

The Most Effective Ways To Spot A Predator Of Any Kind

It's commonly said that knowledge is power, or in other words, the more a person knows, the more successful and productive they will be throughout their endeavors or in reaching their personal and professional goals. The same is true for those interested in Dark Psychology, its affect the human mind and particularly how to identify predators in their surroundings or personal life. Some of the most prolific shared traits of predatory people include:

- An uncanny ability to fake their emotions depending on their situation or audience, but no actual empathy or emotional connections are formed
- They tend to embrace the victim role when they are in trouble or in a setting where they are receiving negative attention. Playing people's emotions by increasing the amount of pity someone feels for them or the other person's guilt about getting angry at the predatory individual is the type of emotional control they seek in social, personal and work environments
- They refuse to take responsibility for their actions (with regards to how they affect others or even how they affect the individual). Depending on the situation, many

predators will blame the victim for their issues or negative emotional experiences while boosting their own image as the victim of the event

- Their personal opinion of themselves is very low and uncomfortably negative. That is why predators are often known for hiding behind carefully constructed psychological masks that show the people that they interact with on a daily basis (or their victims if they are on a hunt) so that people are often caught by surprise when they finally see the individual for who and what they are

Pro Tip: Know How To Determine Your Psychological Personality Types On Sight

It may seem overwhelming to those just starting to explore the area of psychology, but particularly for those peeling away the layers of Dark Psychology, the more you know about the topic, the minute sections that make it so worthy of long-term study, and any branch of the general field that connects with your interests, the better off you will be. The amount of knowledge collected before practical use affects whether a person is able to comprehend Dark Psychology traits as regular behavior and how well they will be able to identify them in their daily interactions (if at all).

One of the best topics to cover when collecting your base knowledge of psychology and how it affects human behavior is the established Psychological Personality Types and what to look for when you're trying to categorize someone you're interacting with. There are a number of different actions, twitches, eye movements or word choices people can make that are controlled by their personality type and history of behavioral patterns. The more you know how to spot and translate these physical and verbal giveaways, the better you will be able to read the people around you to understand their point of view or thought process in different circumstances to help predict their actions (particularly if the situation is concerning or dangerous).

Once individual traits have been identified, people can be classified into a few main Psychological Personality Types. These labels for personalities have entered into mainstream society and are widely recognized even in basic social situations. Here is a brief introduction to Introverts, Extroverts and those with Open Personalities to give everyone a closer look and a better understanding of social human nature.

- **Introverts:** This personality type often comes across as shy and quiet compared to those around them. Ideally, most introverts avoid social situations unless they are necessary and turn their thoughts and reactions inwardly when it comes to dealing with emotions or difficult situations. They can often be labeled as anti-social and do meet some of the character traits required to psychologically meet that label. They are most often provoked by fear as their main psychological drive. This could be fear of rejection or feeling like an outcast, the specifics are different for each introvert based on their personal history, settings and situation.
  - Social anxiety can be a powerful drive for introverts and when this is the case, their anxieties in social situations can manifest as physical ticks such as finger drumming, wringing of the hands or chewing on their lip.
  - There are not a lot of introverts that fit easily into the Dark Psychology field of study. Those who do qualify both as introverts and as dark characters tend to lean heavily toward narcissism and the characteristics that come with that label.
  - Introverts are known to get fatigued during group activities or when surrounded by a large number of people (particularly if they are not used to being in

larger groups). One of the reasons for this is due to their natural instinct to remain inside their own heads, focus on keeping their defenses up and protect themselves from drawing any attention from the people around them

- o One of the positive characteristics of introverts is that they are observant and specific with regards to their environments. Since they spend most of their time in defensive mode, they are always absorbing information and taking mental images of their surroundings to recall if the situation needs it.

- **Extroverts:** This Psychological Personality Type is best known for being outgoing, welcoming and loud speakers. While this may be true in the case of many individuals, not all extroverts have the same open nature and research has shown that they are more likely to exhibit dangerous Dark Psychology traits in their personal behavior than other personalities. Again, this depends on their individual history, health status and surroundings. Like with introverts, people who qualify as extroverts can also display physical characteristics or behavioral patterns such as:
  - o High levels of confidence that can be interpreted through their posture typically through squared

shoulders, holding their head high and keeping their core tight

- o Extroverts are better at making direct eye contact in conversation, which can be tricky when it comes to dealing with extroverts who are well-practiced in techniques like persuasion and manipulation as they are more likely to be able to deliver falsehoods while also holding direct eye contact
- o A firm handshake is one of the physical characteristics that can be associated with extroverts as handshakes are typically connected to self-confidence levels so that the more confidence a person has in themselves, the more solid and firm their handshake with will be
- o Extroverts can sometimes be classified as aggressive as they are more prone to violence or shouting than other personalities

- **Open Personality:** People with open personalities typically display all of the positive psychological traits of both introverts and extroverts without the extremes that can hinder the social skills of those other personality types. Of the personality types, they are typically the most social with large groups of friends (not all of them close, some maybe just acquaintances) and make excellent additions to teams and group assignments. People with open personalities are highly adaptable and are known for finding a way to feel comfortable in any situation they find themselves in.

- o Open personalities are welcoming of new experiences which can play in their favor throughout life if used properly but can also be difficult for them at times as their widespread interest can also be a form of distraction. This type of person tends to know a little about a lot of different topics so they are great to have around for trivia nights or as an on-call handyperson. This wide range of knowledge can hinder their interest in focusing on one field of study or professional practice

- o People with open personalities do not just like to attend parties and other social events, but also like to be the one throwing them. They do best (personally and professionally) when they have people around them either for support or as an audience

- o There are some physical characteristics associated with open personalities such as a warm and wide smile that many would make note of on their first meeting or making physical contact when they communicate with others

There are other, lesser known Psychological Personality Types that are not as well-studied or often diagnosed as those listed above. This includes the Diligent Personality Type (which is characterized by high levels of energy that can border on aggressive or dominating) and the Neurotic Personality Type (often characterized by their anxious, repetitive and sometimes compulsive behavioral patterns). What has been discovered about these personality types is that they are less likely to be identified without also displaying some psychological disorders related to their emotional control or communication.

For more information on Psychological Personality Types, psychological masks, their determining factors and all of the other traits involved in identifying people by their personality characteristics, check out *How To Analyze People By Sight: The Ultimate Guide To Read Anyone Like A Magician In 5 Minutes, Handle Your Relations & Instantly Read Body Language With Dark Psychology*, our ultimate guide on Dark Psychology, self-analyzing and analyzing everyone your encounter by sight!

A Few Different Types Of Predatory Behavior

In order to fit into a specific category and be treated or contained as a dangerous predatory personality, someone has to display at least three or more of the traits associated with their particular type and be diagnosed by a professional psychologist or another expert that is trained and accredited at labeling predators. However, just because someone is not a predator by Psychological Personality Type or traits, it does not mean that a person cannot exhibit predatory behaviors.

Here is a look at some of the most recognized and widely practiced predatory behaviors acknowledged by experts across the globe. There are four main behaviors that have been identified in predators who take advantage of their knowledge and practical experience with Dark Psychology in order to victimize others:

- **Violence:** Whether it is physical, emotional or psychological, predators with aggressive personalities or lack of emotional control when it comes to their personal feelings have a habit of taking their reactions, thoughts or decisions to a level of violent energy that is rarely called for in the situation. Lack of reasonable thinking or inability to calm oneself down in stressful situations are two of the most common traits associated with predators that exhibit violent behaviors.

- **Eerie Calmness:** Having the emotional control and self-awareness that helps people make rational decisions in high-stress situations is something that most adults have a basic understanding and talent with by the time they are out of school and in the professional world, but it is never something that people stop practicing and honing their abilities for. A flat and unemotional response to settings and events that call for it, replaced or overtaken by a sense of calmness and control that can make others around them uncomfortable, is a type of behavior that is often associated with Social Predators, Emotional Predators and predators that may also be classified as introverted when studied by psychological professionals.

- **Rationality & Understanding:** Predators who display leadership and charismatic traits in social settings and in their behavioral patterns typically also have the ability to maintain control over their personal emotions and reactions regardless of changes to their settings or circumstances. They do not act impulsively and take pride in their ability to come up with rational and logical solutions to problems that others may have given up on or dismissed as a loss. They have a solid understanding of how things around them work, whether it is the social circles of their office or choosing an argument to bring a customer to their way of thinking. When used productively, these talents can be very helpful in professional endeavors.

- **Control & Dominance:** Often also seen alongside interactive behaviors in violent predators, these types of people are often stubborn and do not work well with others unless they have absolute control over the situation. In environments or assignments where they do not have total control, predators with this type of behavioral pattern will do everything they can to make themselves indispensable or improve their standing, even if it means tearing down and causing harm to others at the same time.

Dark Psychology, Predators & Deception: The Methods For Use & Protection

The shadowy name may make some people want to avoid talking about it or at least hesitate before trying to understand the concept, but the truth is that many of the tactics, techniques, and theories of Dark Psychology are in use (sometimes intentionally, but many times unconsciously) in each person's daily interactions with everyone they come into contact with and regular communications with other people they have stronger connections with from friends and family to clients or even perfect strangers at the point of introduction.

At its core, Dark Psychology is the categorized and published study of the more wicked side to human nature, thoughts and behavioral patterns: what defines it, how to observe it, what to look for in people (from their appearance to the things they say in everyday conversations), where the lines are considering morality and ethics and how it can be used for both beneficial and malevolent purposes.

Predators are just one category of Dark Psychology studies and are known for their talents with psychological deception and coercion. Using popular methods of deception and collecting as much information on their potential victims before making initial contact is typically the first course of action for predators (regardless of their specific subcategory or predatory characteristics).

What Is The Art Of Deception?

Once they have picked out their victim, the next step for them is to earn the victim's trust and then use methods of deception in order to gain control of them to achieve their goal. Defined, deception is the act of deceiving someone or making them believe or even support a statement or other information that is not true. When it goes from being a simple action to being classified as art, someone has practiced and developed their deceptive skills to a point that their act is seamless, watertight, and effective for achieving the goals they designed them for.

Common examples of deception people may run into in their daily lives include:

- Children are good at mild deception, particularly when they feel they are in trouble or know they have done something wrong. One of the most used deceptive techniques used by children is the "upset stomach" or "painful belly". By feigning an illness that is bad enough to prevent them from doing or talking about whatever they are trying to avoid, they learn that as long as they do not have to claim anything bad enough that it would need a doctor, they can use this as an effective means of deception for a variety of circumstances (assuming they do not get caught).
- The ethics of medical studies and the use of placebos has been called into question on whether or not it is right, effective for getting reliable results, or a method of research that should be considered because of the deceptive nature and potential effect on the results. A

placebo is a sugar-based pill that is labeled as another type of legitimate medicine that is being tested and given to half of the test subjects at the same frequency of the medicated half to see how the chemical make-up of the actual medicine affects the human form compared to the effects felt by those taking the placebo.

- The "Little White Lie" is another common deceptive technique that people use for a variety of reasons. A little white lie a statement that is untrue or deceptive but said in order to prevent the harmful emotional or psychological effects that the truth would have on an individual. Examples of this include telling a co-worker that you like the new outfit they're wearing as a way of boosting their confidence even though it may not be a style you enjoy or telling a client that the ridiculous amount of detail work they had you do to close a sale was no problem even though you had to put in three hours of overtime.

Predators of any kind are dangerous as their main goal in life is to cause harm to others for their own self-satisfaction, elevation or improvement. For those who see these behaviors or character-defining traits in their friends, loved ones or the people they work with, the only way to ensure you are safe from the grasp of a predator and keep from becoming a victim is to remove them or yourself from any closeness or familiarity with them. It can be more difficult than it sounds, depending on close you are to the person or how limited you are in actions you can take to control the situation, but it is well worth it, in the end, to guarantee the preservation of your own psychology, mental and emotional status throughout all of life's ups and downs.

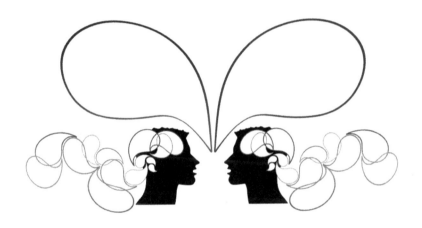

Ways To Spot Deception: Tips From Investigative Teams & Seasoned Police Officers

- **Quiet & Observant:** This is a shared quality of predators and those who use Dark Psychology techniques in order to further their personal or professional standing. The main reason for this is that in order to find weaknesses and vulnerabilities in people, projects or situations, you have to have a solid understanding of what is happening around you. The more information a person can gather about their surroundings or the people that they are involved with, the more they have to use to their benefit when the time comes. People who use blackmail as a way of obtaining money or run cons are known for being good listeners and careful watchers by those who knew them before or during their criminal acts. These types of people are often described as being introverts due to their reserved nature, but actually fit more closely into the Open Personality category as they can move freely between introverted and extroverted depending on what their current needs are.
  - **The Danger Is In The Details:** Predators that deal in cons or social ruses such as theft from targeted events rely on deception and falsehoods in order to avoid getting caught or hindered in their plans. Studies done on an international scale and over a variety of age groups show that one behavioral habit of people that have honed

their skills in duplicity is that when they have to lie in order to achieve their goals, they put in as few details as possible. For example, they may tell someone that they can't meet up with them later because they're going out, but they will leave out details like what time they will be out or where specifically they will be going. The reason for this is because details can be checked and they can be contested.

- **Keep It Simple & Straightforward:** The best advice most experts offer to those looking to develop their powers of deception is not to willingly or openly provide information or details about anything you're doing. Only inform people of what is happening when they ask and make sure to only answer what they ask. Keep it vague and keep it simple. More complex stories are more difficult to remember and far easier to get caught in if they are false.

- **Repetition & Buying Time:** It may make someone sound like a parrot if they are being interviewed or interrogated, but one behavioral habit that those who practice Dark Psychology either come by naturally or learn as a survival skill is the act of repeating questions they are asked before answering them or repeating important bits of information (often in their own words) to ensure there is no misunderstanding and also to make sure that they only respond to exactly what has been asked of them. This way they can avoid accidentally letting any additional or possible damning information slip.

- o Repetition is another behavioral habit shared by those who also exhibit traits of psychopathy and still developing social skills. When used by these types of personalities, repetition can also be classified as mimicry. In repeating the tone and the exact wording of those who speak to them first, they are able to practice their own tone and wording as they develop a personal style and flair that will come into play in their more complex Dark Psychology techniques and plans. Not only are they gaining practical experience with this behavioral trait, but they can also be sure that the style they're developing is natural compared to other human behavioral and social characteristics.

- **Physical Ticks & Giveaways:** When asked their thoughts on an emotional topic or asked their feelings about something personal and sensitive, deceptive people tend to take comfort in unconscious physical ticks that can be used as giveaways for those observing for deceptive traits. Some of the most noted deceptive ticks include:

- o Playing with their hair either by twirling it in their fingers or running their hands through it to brush it away from their face (even if there isn't anything there)
- o Increased heart rate and heavier breathing are also common signs of deception
- o Fiddling with buttons or pulling at their clothes when thinking or listening carefully to what is being discussed but do not want to make eye contact with the people around them
- o The individual movements or habits that people show will vary from person to person the key to mastering the art of detecting deception is practicing your observing and socializing skills

Ready to learn more about Dark Psychology and the different types of techniques people use when practicing or studying this psychological field? Keep reading to learn not only what kind of variety there is of methods and actions to be developed, but also how to identify these techniques when they are used on you and how to protect yourself from becoming a victim of predatory behavior.

Chapter 3: The Dark Psychology Of Persuasion & How To Handle It In Any Setting

As a common communication skill, there is nothing fundamentally wrong with the art of persuasion. After all, that's how we convince people to support our causes or to join our side of an argument. Sales representatives in every industry use persuasion tactics to promote their products over their competitors and politicians use them to bring voters to their side before an election. Wanting others to be on our side is a natural human emotion related to our primal need for socialization with others, having people around us that we now have our backs and being liked by those who may have jumped to negative conclusions based on appearance or the unusual events of a situation that may have given them a bad first impression.

However, when used for nefarious or malevolent purposes, persuasion takes a different turn and becomes a dangerous tool for coercion and taking advantage of others. This is where even a basic understanding of Dark and Covert Persuasion tactics can come in handy for those who have struggled with falling for good persuasion strategies in the past. In this chapter, we'll take a closer look at persuasion as a psychological method of control and as a whole so that readers have a better grasp of persuasion from the definition and concept to identification and protection.

What Is Persuasion?

Persuasion is defined as the intentional process of influencing others by providing information, forming a campaign or visual stimulant that designed to alter their thoughts and feelings, or through subtle coercion. In some cases, the coercion is subliminal and really it has to be in order for persuasion to be fully effective. People can try to persuade other people that they are in the right or that they know the best way to accomplish a task, but just telling others (even supported by facts, experience, and knowledge) can lead to arguments and resentment. The key to persuasion is being able to get someone to persuade themselves using the arguments, information or images they've been presented with by the person trying to do the persuading.

Dark Psychology: The Difference In Dark Persuasion & General Psychological Persuasion

Dark Persuasion is a popular topic for people studying Dark Psychology simply because of how prevalent persuasion is in daily global communications. Dark Persuasion is also defined as the act of getting someone to do, think, feel or believe something through convincing them with information and arguments or by endearing them to a concept or topic through emotional appeals. The difference between Dark Persuasion and persuasion in general psychology is the motive and drive behind the need to persuade alongside the overall goal and intention of the person doing the persuading.

In other words, people who practice general persuasion tactics may not have any kind of underlying motive for their campaigns. This is common in the advertising industry as people who are good at persuasion are hired to convince people of something or to buy something, but never with any actual intent for further control or manipulation. The difference can be difficult to see, particularly for those who are themselves inexperienced with persuasion techniques or up against someone who has mastered (or come close to mastering) the art of persuasion. One trick for those who think they may be under the influence of someone practicing Dark Persuasion is to take a step back and look at the situation to see if there is a potential bigger picture at play. General psychological persuasion usually only has one goal: win someone over so they buy your product, take up a cause or join your side in an argument. Dark Persuasion will always take plans and techniques a step further.

Those who practice and rely on Dark Persuasion tactics and methods never just want someone to change their minds and leave it at that. There is always a further drive or intention behind their persuasion tactics. This can be anything from ensuring their support when others try to confront them or in order to get them to take action that they themselves want to avoid because it is dangerous or immoral and could hurt their own reputation. The basics are that, like with most areas of

Dark Psychology, people who practice Dark Persuasion see other people as tools or as a means to an end in order to better their lives or their standing.

What Is Dark Persuasion Versus Covert Persuasion?

The word "covert" has a way of making people instantly suspicious and hesitant to part in situations or methods. Others automatically think about super spies like James Bond and the covert operations such characters are famous for. The definition of covert is a thought, technique or action that is performed without any direct acknowledgment or with any witness or actual sight.

Covert Persuasion has no moral or ethical issues or motives, as with Dark Persuasion, but instead covers those techniques for general persuasion that target their audience's ability to persuade them over to their side without them ever knowing they had been the target of a successful persuasion campaign and made up their own minds instead. While people who practice Dark Persuasion can use techniques identified and included in the art of Covert Persuasion, the covert methods on their own are not considered dark or unethical. Distinguishing the difference between the two comes down to being able to determine motive and intent behind the persuasion techniques. Ask yourself these questions when you think you're being persuaded or when you feel compelled to change your mind (and are not quite sure why):

- Is it dangerous or potentially harmful in any way?
- Who benefits from this? Is there any person specifically or could it potentially benefit a larger group of people?
- Do I trust this person and how they are speaking to me or presenting their argument?
  - Have they said anything painful or insulting?

- - Have they done or said anything that targeted your self-esteem or opinion of yourself?
- Do I have the information I need to make an informed decision?
  - What other information should I look for before taking any kind of action in this matter?

Common Situations For Potentially Dark Persuasive Behavior To Thrive

One method of persuasion (Dark, Covert or otherwise) is the agreement method. This technique sits at the very core of psychological persuasion studies and is a good starting exercise for those new to the art of persuasion to make a habit of. Basically, once the target has been identified, the goal has been determined and a plan has been enacted, the next course of action for someone trying to persuade others is to agree with every word that comes out of their mouths. Even if it is counterintuitive to getting them on your side, agreeing with people builds trust (a critical element of successful persuasion). The most important rule for those who want to start practicing this method is that the target is always right. Even when you know they are wrong, they are right.

It can sound confusing, but basically what this means that when you are trying to persuade someone of something and they disagree with you or say something incorrect, instead of confronting them or calling them out on it and telling them what is correct or what you want them to believe, you find a way to alter their way of thinking first by agreeing with them and then employing other subtle persuasion techniques to get them to change their point of view. The person disagreeing with the persuader or saying something that is contradictory to the ultimate goal of the persuasion plan is a clear sign that the persuasion methods employed so far have not been successful and the plan may need altering. This is where having a mental toolbox filled with persuasion tactics is good (even crucial) for those who use it or want to start practicing it in their own lives.

Technological developments are of particular interest to those who practice persuasive behavior. The main reasons for this are that technology (bought for personal or professional use) is around us at all times. From cell phones in everyone's pockets or bags to televisions on the walls in virtually every restaurant, waiting for an area or other space where people gather to pass time together or on their own. This is also one of the reasons that the advertising industry is such a popular destination for those who know they have a talent for persuasion. When it comes to sharing videos, images or news clips, nothing travels faster than a funny ad or celebrity endorsement shared on social media or sent as a private message for people to share with friends and family.

Technology has opened the world for the persuasive (and predators of all kinds) and made it easier for them to expand their target audiences and general hunting grounds. The good news for potential victims is that a larger collection of people to prey on means a more diverse and contradicting collection of people they need to win over. This means that persuasive people have new challenges, not in actually reaching people as that has become one of the easiest parts of any Dark Psychological control method thanks to constant internet access and mobile technology, but actually winning people over as one campaign or argument may not connect with some the way it does with others.

Popular Persuasion Techniques For Personal Use

One of the most common Covert Persuasion tactics at use in both personal and professional circles is understanding of the "Big Picture". No matter what the situation, the specifics, or the end goal, understanding how the target not only remembers their past experiences but also envisions their future. This tactic is particularly effective for those who have a target that is on the negative side of their argument and need to be persuaded to the positive side to either gain support or close a sale. People are more likely to be open to persuasion and accepting other information or actions as beneficial if they feel the person they're talking to understands them and sees them as an individual (rather than a target). Social skills, communication skills, empathy and the ability to translate words and actions as an individual's emotional responses are all other basic human connection abilities that are good to have experience with when trying to persuade someone.

- Listen to the person's experience and history with the topic you are trying to persuade them on
- Empathize and find some common ground in order to win their trust and make a personal connection
- Always ask them where they stand and why they feel that way about your topic before trying any persuasion techniques. This is a way of creating a baseline or a starting point to simplify building an effective persuasion plan
- Once their stance has been established, ask them about how they see the situation or argument wrapping up. This lets you know which potential future they are envisioning and how their ideal situation would end
- Now that you have an understanding of their history and their vision of the future (as it relates to your topic),

you can choose which more advanced, covert or darker persuasion techniques can help you achieve your ultimate goals and resolve the situation with the future you have envisioned or hoped for

The following chart provides a visual display of how persuasion works at its most elemental level from the starting point (or likelihood of conversion) to the two main paths a person can decide to take from that point in order to change someone's mind to their way of thinking or until the other person takes the actions that the persuader is hoping for.

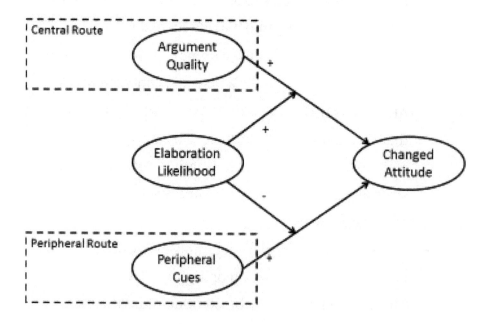

Pro Tip: Use The Past To Influence A Person's Future Actions Or Decisions

The best example of this tip in action comes from the world of competition and sporting events. Most sporting events are split into two halves or have some kind of multiple sections that teams or individuals have to perform efficiently to be named the winner and beat out their competitors or competing teams. When the first half or first part of a challenge does not go well, it does not necessarily mean that the entire game is lost. It is easy to get discouraged when things are not going as planned or someone is not performing as they hoped, particularly if they have been training for some time.

This is when coaches have the opportunity to exercise their persuasion abilities as a means of reigniting a passion or drive for the sport in their disenchanted competitors before the rest of the challenge or competition.

- A common argument for this is that not performing well at the beginning should only serve as more inspiration to boost one's energy and center one's focus more intensely for the rest of the challenge. A renewed drive and improved energy levels (from stretching out sore muscles, rehydrating or consuming some protein or other fuel) can make all the difference in someone's performance and depend on how far behind the person or team is, it can be the determining factor for how to close the gap and then surpass their competitors in order to win the award or game!

If there is more than one potential outcome for the person being persuaded, either by making a decision about a purchase, another person or a course of action, and both of them are equally beneficial for themselves or for the persuader (depending on their motives and intent) one technique those with persuasion experience rely on is moving the target's attention between options so they do not form an emotional or psychological connection to one of them in particular. Even if there is no loss for the person regardless of which decision they make, people tend to feel a sense of loss and regret that can make them start to question the decision they made and how they arrived at it. This is something that is good for people becoming self-aware and seeing that they have been the victims of a persuasive plan or campaign, but not good for those practicing and honing their persuasion techniques.

How To Protect Yourself From Dark Persuasion & The People That Rely On It

At some point, everyone thinks that they are immune to persuasion, that they are either so good at reading people that they would never fall for a shallow pitch or that they are so certain in their thoughts, feelings, and beliefs that they could never be swayed. However, the truth is that at some point in their lives, everyone gets persuaded into changing their mind about something whether it is by a friend who is trying to convince them to see an argument from their point of view (and does so successfully) or a persuasive advertising campaign that wins them over from a brand they've been loyal to for years.

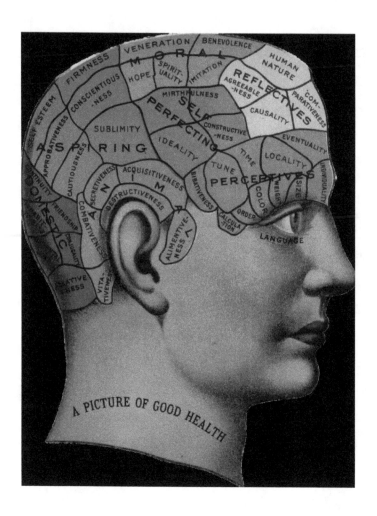

A PICTURE OF GOOD HEALTH

Pro Tip: It Is Better To Be Certain Than To Be Liked

The need to be liked is something that the majority of humanity struggles with at some point in their lives. We are particularly prone to changing our thoughts, beliefs or behaviors in times of stress or solitude, when we find ourselves in new surroundings with new people (particularly if they are a new kind of person than we are accustomed to dealing and socializing with on a regular basis), and throughout maturity from childhood to the early years of adulthood. Many people acknowledge that they have done this at some point, usually in the middle or high school when peer pressure gets the better of most people. It is much easier to recognize and regret after the fact that it is to identify and alter your actions at the moment.

This is a natural human quality that people who use persuasion for darker purposes rely on, particularly if they are having difficulty charming their way into a person's trust and confidences. One of the main causes of the need to be liked is low self-esteem or negative personal opinion of oneself. This is an emotional weakness that makes each person vulnerable to malicious persuasion tactics but can be taken into personal control and dealt with when a person understands what it is about themselves or their lives that is causing such a low opinion.

The main way to do this (and to avoid becoming the victim of a persuasion operation) is by practicing confidence building exercises in order to strengthen your belief in yourself and always have a mind hungry for learning. This last part is important as another cause of low self-worth and faulty self-reliance is often due to a lack of information about a topic or a person that we know little to nothing about. All people form opinions based on what they see and hear on a daily basis, and depending on their Psychological Personality Type, they may be more prone to voicing their thoughts or opinions without knowing the full story. This not only makes people vulnerable to negative comments from others and embarrassment if others who have more knowledge are confrontational with them and they are not prepared, but it is also a factor that those who know how to use persuasion as a weapon or method of control look for in the people they target.

No matter where you look, there is some form of persuasion being used and the majority of it is harmless and has the potential to be used to benefit the whole of society if employed with positive motives. When it comes to persuasion, it is really only the dangerous factors and hints that you should be looking for, the parts of persuasion that can be used as a means of control or attaining power over others. Here are some of the main elements to look for when you think you're the victim of malicious persuasion tactics and how to handle them when they've been identified.

- Is the person or campaign targeting you to make you feel above average or special in any way?

- This in itself may not be a marker of persuasive techniques, but it is one of the most common methods put into effect. By making someone feel special, it boosts their confidence and earns their trust, making them more open to persuasive techniques.

- Are they making contradictory statements or constantly drawing you back to the subject when you try to change the topic of conversation?
  - This is a sign that someone may be trying the positive agreement method in order to gain trust and is subtly trying to keep you focused on their persuasion plan without actually acknowledging or admitting that they are trying to control your thoughts and opinions.

- Do I buy this story they are sharing about the topic? Does it seem like something that is real?
  - Storytelling is a powerful persuasion tool for anyone who wants to make an emotional connection with their target, especially if it is someone they do not know personally. There is nothing that unites people like a good story and a good story can be difficult to see as a persuasion method, especially for those who are just socializing and do not even think they are being influenced.

The majority of knowledge collected, confidence in your personal abilities (whether it is for persuasion or for seeing persuasion tactics for what they are) and level of persuasion skills will come with experience and increased self-awareness. There is no limit of information and research on persuasion in general psychology and Dark Psychology circles. Hopefully, our guide has provided you with everything you need to get started with your personal goals for persuasion (regardless of what they may be), but never stop learning and always seek out more! This is the best way to increase your skill set and knowledge of any topic or practice you take an interest in throughout your life.

Chapter 4: Defining Dark Manipulation & The Character Of A Master Manipulator

Master Manipulators, like those who practice the art of persuasion, have many different levels, intensities, motives and uses for their particular skills that vary from person to person. At the simplest level, manipulators are people who can change their personality, their personability, their opinions or their point of view in order to make someone else believe something that is not true to the point of taking action or making statements that they would never do without influence and not even questioning it.

Psychologists all over the world believe that each person has three psychological faces or sides to their personality that define their individuality, determine their actions and form the basis for all personal connections and relationships started throughout their lifetime:

- The first face that people see when they look at someone is their open face, also sometimes called their public face. This personality is the one they want people to see, the mask they are hiding behind to avoid their personal troubles or protect themselves from emotional harm caused by the rejection or bullying of others around them.

- The second face is the one that only those closest to a person get to know or even get to see. This is the version of ourselves that is more open and honest thanks to the security we feel around those we're most comfortable with. However, it is also part of a mask that people use in order to project the personality we want our closest connections to embrace. Getting past this mask is the only way to build long-lasting and unbreakable personal relationships and this is the mask that is rarely shown by manipulators, even when they are not behaving in a manipulative way around the people they know and love.

- The third (and most evasive) face is the one that no one sees or ever gets to know, sometimes it's the face we don't even show ourselves out of fear or denial. This third face is the one that holds the absolute truths of our personalities and when analyzed (personally or in psychological treatment), can even provide the answers to those who are struggling with discovering who they are, what they stand for, what they believe and who they want to be. It is completely hidden by the psychological masks developed for the other two faces. It is not until the final face has been acknowledged and understood by each person that they can work on getting rid of their surface psychological masks on the first two levels and allow themselves and others to see them as they truly are.

- o When it comes to this side of their individual personalities, those who are manipulators or practicing their manipulation skills will want to become aware of their motives, drives, and goals connected with their true being. The reason for this is that the better understanding a person has of themselves, the more self-aware they are, the better manipulative masks they are able to create because they have a better grasp of their own nature and can better spot (or even predict) emotional responses that could affect their progression or control over the situation they find themselves in.

Being able to use manipulative techniques for personal gain or being able to spot a manipulator in order to avoid becoming a victim or potential target starts with a complete understanding of manipulation as a concept, as a practice, as a character development tool for maturing personalities and the different types manipulation theories and techniques at work in modern society.

In this chapter, we will be covering these topics along with discussing other important information related to manipulation, psychology and the darker side of human influence for personal use or personal protection (depending on your intent and motives).

What Is Manipulation In Psychology?

The definition of manipulation differs depending on who is doing the defining. Most often, it is defined as the act of getting someone to do or say something through clever and skillful influencing on the part of the manipulator. Some definitions even go as far as to list some of the most noticeable traits and patterns of psychological manipulation on that must be present in an individual's behavior with their targets or victims for them to deserve the label as a manipulator, such as:

- Undue pressuring to the point of guilt or discomfort on the part of the victim
- Mental, emotional and psychological distortion to gain control over thoughts and actions
- Circumstantial and personal exploitation (or taking advantage of any weakness or opening they find in a person or situation)

Regardless of who you are talking to and their personal experience with manipulation and manipulation techniques, the majority of people automatically connect the word with negative actions and sometimes even cruel methods of influence that cause pain to others and trick them into doing things they would never do. In some cases, this point of view is accurate and in studying the history of manipulation throughout the human experience, anyone can see why. Mainly it is because of how dark and dangerous manipulative people have proven to be in hindsight when experiences are analyzed, and people are trying to regain control of their lives or mental and psychological state.

When it comes down to it, manipulation (with regards to human psychology) is a means of gaining control over someone else to achieve a certain goal without them becoming aware of any outside persuasion or coercion.

Is There A Difference Between Manipulation & Persuasion?

The difference between manipulation and persuasion lies at their very core and the elements that make them what they are. As we learned in the previous chapter, persuasion is the process of changing someone's beliefs, thoughts or feelings in order to gain their support or get them to take a certain action. The definitions sound almost identical, so how do you tell the difference between persuasion and manipulation when different tactics are identifiable and being employed around you?

Persuasion and manipulation can sometimes be confused as the same concept or two sides of the same coin. The truth is that, at their core, persuasion and manipulation are two completely different psychological tactics that can be employed for both positive and negative results, depending on the person using them and how they decide to benefit from them.

Persuasion is one technique that can be employed to encourage someone into taking an action they were resisting or against at first. This is often done through presenting someone with facts about the situation in question such as reminding your friend they have to work in the morning when it starts to get late at a social event and they are reaching a point of over intoxication.

Manipulation on the other hand, is a series of techniques and tactics formed into a carefully laid out plan to get someone (or a group of people) to change their thoughts, feelings or behaviors. Definitions of manipulation often include words like *clever* and *skillful*, referring to the underhanded, unscrupulous and cunning nature of those who practice this type of Dark Psychology.

What Is Covert Manipulation?

Covert Manipulation, like Covert Persuasion, is often defined as the methods and techniques manipulators use that cannot be identified or even recognized at the moment due to their subtly or due to the personal skills of the manipulator themselves. Some people take up manipulation as their profession, often ending up in criminal or psychologically damaging (to themselves and others) endeavors that solidify their reputation as Master Manipulators as they perfect their skills, abilities, and collection of effective techniques.

Dark Psychology: What Is Dark Manipulation?

Dark Manipulation takes the shady and often underhanded motives of general and covert manipulation techniques and blends them with other methods, theories and aspects of Dark Psychology with the intention of causing harm to others, creating chaos in their environment and doing so for reasons ranging from their own pleasure and entertainment to their own benefit and promotion. It can be difficult to see the difference (sometimes impossible, depending on the techniques employed and the skill of the individual at using them to manipulate others) and is often only identified after the fact when the victims of manipulation have to face consequences of their actions and decisions or are trying to recover from negative repercussions of the situation they were manipulated into or within.

The Characteristics Of A Master Manipulator

The best way to be able to protect yourself from being the target of manipulation is to know how to spot a Master Manipulator before they get the chance to make you just another victim of their self-serving plans. Most manipulative people prefer the subtle and calculated approach. These people often show signs of psychopathy, sociopathy, and narcissism. There is also a smaller, but equally malicious group of Master Manipulators who embrace more aggressive (sometimes violent) manipulation techniques that are easy to spot when encountered, but the difficulty with this type of manipulation is that by the time a person is bold enough to use obvious manipulation methods on someone else, that person is already too deeply involved with the manipulator or their plan to be able to break away without circumstantial consequences like repercussions at work or fracturing of the home life or personal damage (physically, mentally, emotionally or psychologically). The sad truth is that regardless of which type of Master Manipulator people find themselves up against, by the time most manipulation victims realize that something is wrong, it is too late to escape the situation without having to take time to recover or rebuild their lives and relationships.

One of the most notable characteristics of a Master Manipulator is their ability to design and hide behind psychological masks in order to win people's trust or create some common ground for a seemingly deeper emotional connection with the target from their point of view. Psychological masks typically start to form during puberty and other major changes in life when people start to alter aspects of their personality (knowingly or unknowingly). By adulthood, most people are starting to break through their personal masks through increased self-awareness, greater emotional maturity, psychological stability, and adapted social skills and abilities practiced throughout their life to this point.

Unless, of course, the person has intentionally formed a psychological mask to wear as a means of manipulating others.

Here is a closer look at a couple of the most common Psychological Personality Masks perfected and worn by those studying the art of manipulation:

- **The People Pleaser:** People Pleasers base their fundamental opinion of themselves on how others see, describe and feel about them. Instead of forming their own opinions and voicing them around others, they listen and agree with the popular opinions shared by those around them so that they always have friends and supportive connections regardless of where they are. Manipulators take this to the next step and put their People Pleaser mask on to agree with everyone they talk to, especially if they need the person they're winning over to do something for them.
  - o This can be a dangerous tactic for manipulators with large social circles or groups of people around them (from co-workers to friends and family). It becomes even riskier when the people around them are diverse and resides on opposite ends of the spectrum when it comes to choosing their sides on any given subject. If the manipulator agrees with one person and then is

heard agreeing with someone else of the opposite opinion, they've just trapped themselves in a situation where they can be considered a liar and lose the trust they rely on so intensely in order to get people to do what they need.

- **The Hero Mask:** This is a more direct and confident mask that manipulators wear. Those who wear this mask need to feel like the hero or the one who is needed in any given situation and is common in the professional world. However, manipulators thrive on having other people do things for them so the ones who also have a heroism complex (and can manage the two successfully) have developed their own methods of being considered the hero and getting the credit for accomplishments while convincing those around them to do all the work. The benefit of this is that they are able to fill roles that are beneficial to how others see them and their personal success when a goal is met or a task is finished effectively.
  - This type of mask can also be flipped by experienced manipulators typically don the Hero mask when circumstances are positive and events play out the way they intended with their influence. Thanks to the human element of the situation (free will, imperfections and emotional responses) there is always a chance that a

manipulation technique will backfire, no matter how well it was planned or executed.

o   When this happens, the experienced manipulator knows to flip their Hero mask to reveal the opposite side of its nature, the Martyr mask. This side of the mask paints the wearer as the victim in order to draw pity and distract attention from their role in the course of events or as a way to lessen the severity of their consequences for failure. For manipulators, this side of the mask has been designed not only to earn pity but to completely shift responsibility for the failings on the person they were manipulating. They take the blame, the manipulator is given another chance or forgiven based on their lack of control over the other person's actions (as far as the authoritative person is concerned) and the manipulator has just added another beneficial experience to their overall knowledge and practice of Dark Manipulation through the use of Psychological Personality masks.

Due to their need for control, those who were classified as manipulators psychologically tend to prefer their own company or create a group of people around them that have lower confidence or are more introverted. This means that it is rare to find a group of manipulative people working together. Another reason for this is that Master Manipulators are typically only concerned in their own benefit and promotion regardless of the harm it may do to others, even though they need that person or those people in order to achieve their ultimate goal, whatever that might be at the time. Manipulators tend to be drawn to leadership positions because they have a talent for getting people to do whatever they are told or invited to join in on, as long as it does not put the manipulative person at any risk or threaten their standing in the environment (whether it is work, home or in social settings).

Popular Manipulation Techniques At Work In People's Daily Lives

When Master Manipulators target others for emotional, romantic or other social purposes and find someone they are ready to work their magic on, their first step is to win their trust and lay the foundations of personal connection. Even though they are shallow on the side of the manipulative person, their target will have no doubts that they truly feel the emotions they describe or thinking the thoughts they are sharing in order to gain and hold their trust. This is a common and repetitive trait amongst all of the personalities, predatory types, manipulators and other groups of people whose actions and behaviors have become the study of Dark Psychology. Since their goals and intentions require the assistance of other people who do not even realize they are being influenced and controlled, the first techniques Master Manipulators have to research, choose and perfect through practical use are the ones that focus on earning people's trust through deception and persuasion, all while seeming as genuine and above board as possible.

Pro Tip: Become An Observer (Especially In New Settings With Unfamiliar People)

All Master Manipulators are observers. Even people who may not be considered manipulative by nature (but employ methods of manipulation in their daily lives or have used or relied on them in the past) know the importance of hanging back and watching how others interact with the people around them, in various circumstances or in their specific settings. Gaining an understanding of how their targets think, feel, react and interact with others is critical to the formation of an effective manipulation plan. Observing before making contact gives Master Manipulators the information they need to know so that they can:

- Choose the best way to approach their target and make their initial connection
    - Is the person someone that talks openly and enthusiastically with people they meet? If so, the best initial approach may be the direct one.
    - Is the person someone that tends to avoid other people, particularly in larger groups or interactive situations? If so, the patient approach might be better. Instead of walking up and introducing themselves, a virtual invitation to coffee through social media or by work email may be their best option after the target has known them for at least a few days (long enough to start becoming comfortable around them).
- Choose the right Psychological Personality Mask to wear around them to encourage their cooperation or coercion into getting more deeply involved
    - Do the actions of the target or the way they speak to others suggest that they are the kind of person

needs to be needed? For this type of target, a Master Manipulator would most likely put on their Victim or Helpless Mask so they can get the target to do what they want by making them feel like a hero (even though in hindsight, their words and actions will most likely be interpreted as harmful).

o Does the target consider themselves more of an outcast? In this type of situation, a manipulative person will want to find a way to find some common ground, so the best choice for them is to also project the airs and behavioral patterns of an outcast.

- For example, everyone at the office loves superhero movies, including the Master Manipulator. A new co-worker comes in that the manipulative person sees as a potential target but in observing their behavior finds out the individual is not just a little shy and quiet, avoiding others as best they can. When they are drawn into conversation, they have no trouble voicing their opinions, even taking pride in being the only one in the office who does not like superhero movies.

- The best means of approach for a Master Manipulator in this situation is the one-on-one conversation starter, but only away from other co-workers or people who know they are lying when they tell the target they also are over the superhero movies constantly being put out. They will then even take this opinion a step further as a way of endearing themselves to the target by rolling their eyes and laughing about the television shows, books and games about superheroes and there is just no escaping. The two will share a laugh and the connection will be formed.
- Since the rest of the office has been put off by the new co-worker's hostile attitude to friendly interaction and assertive opinions about the entertainment industry and other topics when someone does approach them, they have set themselves as the perfect target for manipulation by isolating themselves from people who know the Master Manipulator well enough to warn them of the deceptive behavior before it becomes an issue or

while there is still a chance for them to break free of their hold.

- From the view of the target, the manipulative co-worker has shown they have the potential to be a good friend and earned their trust by also behaving like an outcast around them. All the while, the Master Manipulator is carefully monitoring and controlling their daily interactions so that the target does not question this view and the co-workers who have known them for years do not notice a change in their personality or behavior that would serve as a warning that they are not who they claim to be.

- In this type of manipulative situation, it benefits both the Master Manipulator, their potential targets and the people surrounding both of them to harness and rely on their powers of observation. The target especially, as watching all of their co-workers and how they interact with one another before opening themselves up to any of them could have prevented their involvement with a Master Manipulator.

- Choose how best to proceed in order to meet their goals or get whatever it is that they want
  - This means choosing the right methods and techniques for manipulation and forming a plan based on all of the information they've gathered. The more individualized they can make a manipulative pal of action for their target, the greater their chances of success.

Other characteristics of Master Manipulators include:

- Lack of understanding, or understanding but lack of concern, for personal boundaries of any kind
  - Manipulators want nothing more than total control over their victims, along with their thoughts, emotions, and action. The more they can invade and influence their personal space, the more control they feel they have.
- Disloyalty is a big problem with manipulative people
  - They will talk about working as a team and facing every challenge together, saying whatever they must to keep their targets cooperative and enthusiastic about the plan. However, the moment anything goes wrong, or someone interferes with their success, the Master Manipulator has no trouble jumping ship to

preserve their own interests and leaving their target to clean up the mess while taking the blame for all failures or problems created by the manipulation plan of action.

- Master Manipulators enjoy targeting good people (or people that others classify as "good")
    - Everyone has their own opinion of what constitutes a good person, but generally good people are those with optimistic outlooks on life, a helpful attitude in the face of challenges, well-honed empathy and emotional maturity and a general desire to see everyone succeeding.
    - Good people are often the targets of manipulative individuals as they are more open with their communications and are always willing to help out when they can. Manipulative people often describe good people as gullible and trusting, two personality traits they look for in their victims, as it makes them easier to take advantage of.
    - Depending on their personal motives or intent, manipulative people can target good people just for the challenge of getting them to do something bad (after being convinced it is the right or only option) and the enjoyment of witnessing them struggle with their opinion of themselves when

they realize what they've done. This is a common practice for manipulative people who thrive on chaos, particularly if their own life has taken a stagnant or boring turn.

How To Protect Yourself From A Manipulator Or From Manipulation Techniques

It is often said that actions speak louder than words. When it comes to protecting yourself from manipulation, learning to judge the quality of the people around you or the people you come into contact with by how they behave in different situations or with different people over the things they say is the best advice anyone can receive. Manipulative people are the definition of "two-faced" and the most effective way to avoid getting pulled into their selfish plans, need for chaos and self-gratification over anything else is to not be fooled by their carefully chosen words.

One of the best ways to protect yourself from Master Manipulators or anyone who uses manipulative techniques for their own benefit or enjoyment is to always be questioning. This does not mean that it is best not to trust people in general. While many people will try to manipulate others at some point in their lives, the majority of people have been shown by psychology and through years of personality, study to be fundamentally honest and open when they are trying to form a connection to another person or establish their place within a group of people. Most people want to be liked and respected for who they are at their core so that they do not have to put on masks or remember lies about what they do and do not like with different people. This is something that manipulative people take advantage of when they are hunting for targets and the natural desire to trust others that most people experience is also the downfall of many.

To avoid becoming one of those people who sees everything clearly in hindsight after seeing through a manipulative action or having to face the consequences of having an active role in a Master Manipulator's plan, get into the habit of trusting your instincts and asking questions when you have concerns. Be excited when new opportunities come your way but be sure to do your research before accepting an offer, diving right in or going along with someone else's plan. Make new friends and experience socializing with people but get to know them as much as you can by seeing them from other people's points of view and listening to how they talk to and about others.

If you ever grow concerned about your thoughts, feelings and actions and are not certain as to why (particularly if it is something you would have told someone you would never think, feel or do), take a step back and take a look at what you feel, why you are questioning yourself, who else is involved in what's captured your attention, and establish how you feel about your role in everything. If you're feeling that something is off or wrong with what is happening around you, there most likely is and the only way to regain control when you find yourself caught in a manipulative trap is to:

- Observe the situation and figure out what specifically is wrong
- Determine who is involved and who is doing the manipulating
- Remove yourself from the situation, seeking help from others if necessary
- Cease contact with the manipulative person, reporting them to the authorities or to an authoritative figure (like an employer or supervisor) if the situation is severe enough to require further or possibly legal action

Chapter 5: Brainwashing, The Damage It Does & Other Dark Mind Control Techniques

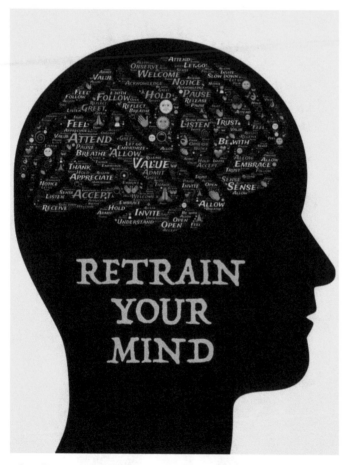

The first recorded use of the term *brainwashing* happened in the 1950s during the Korean War and was quickly popularized as the concept spread fear, paranoia and all other kinds of negative emotions throughout peoples of all races, creeds, and religions around the globe. It was used to describe the process of thought reform and persuasion employed by Korean and Chinese soldiers to affect the mental state of American Prisoners of War under their control. During their time in the foreign prison camps, POWs were put through a variety of brainwashing techniques (most of the experimental and previously untested) until they lost their identities, converted national loyalty against their home country and even admitted to war crimes they no involvement with.

Since its conception and widespread acceptance as a psychological advancement, brainwashing has been a point of interest for many people from the ones wanting to use, the ones wanting to regain their control over themselves and those who want to avoid ever coming into contact with the brainwashing type or their many techniques and intents. While the term and its study may be newer in the realm of psychology, the actual processes and methods employed in brainwashing have been around as long as people have wanted to control the way others think, feel and behave. In this chapter, we'll be taking a closer look at brainwashing, the basics of it and how to keep from becoming a target, particularly of those who intend to do harm.

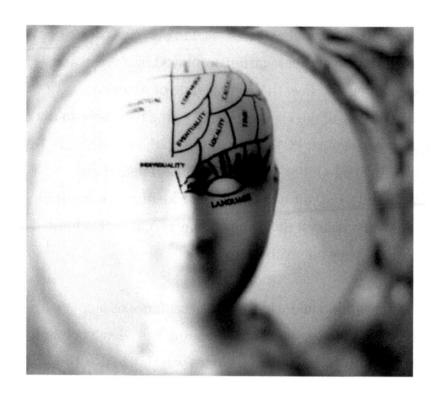

The Basics of Brainwashing: What Is It & How Is It Different From Other Methods Of Psychological Influence?

Brainwashing is not a new concept in psychology or even with regards to human history when you look at the elements of the method and where they developed from. It is sometimes called *thought reform* by those who study it professionally, a title was given to the method thanks to the process involved in brainwashing someone. It is defined as the intentional act of changing the thoughts or feelings of another person or group of people against their will (and sometimes without their knowledge). Brainwashing techniques are in use everywhere you look, and not always for underhanded or dangerous reasons. Some techniques are of regular use in advertising companies or for political campaigns. Like persuasion and manipulation, it is difficult to identify until you are completely absorbed in it. However, unlike those two methods that also have deep roots in psychology and Dark Psychology, brainwashing is less effective unless put to use on large groups and with willing victims (like with cults and political followers).

A quick comparison of methods so those new to the world of Dark Psychology have an easier time distinguishing a difference:

- Persuasion when used aims to get the target to think they've changed their own minds through careful thought and increased knowledge of the situation. People who use this method want their targets to have a change in attitude that makes them feel positive about their decision to change their thoughts or behaviors. They want to influence their future without rewriting their past

- Manipulation is the forceful changing of someone's thoughts and feelings through aggressive pressure as a means of gaining control of their actions for a selfish and often malevolent purpose. They have no interest in their target's past or long-term future, beyond what they need to know to gain power over them for their own benefit.

Brainwashing methods lie somewhere in the middle of the two. They are not always used with vicious intent, although the concept has earned that reputation due to its popularity with those who seek to use it as a means of control or influence over others. The ultimate goal of brainwashing is for the brainwasher (sometimes referred to as the agent) is to get the target to change their thoughts and feelings down to their core beliefs and past experiences in order gain control over how they think and react. When used for wrong or unethical means, the main purpose of brainwashing is to attack a person at their very foundation (their understanding of who they are, their morality and ethical views) and cause them to doubt themselves so they embrace the brainwashing techniques used as truth, reassurance or validation as they try to piece together their lives and the new "truths" they've been exposed to.

More mild versions of brainwashing and effective techniques involved with it have been notably used to sell products like cigarettes by placing subliminal messages in movies, television shows, papers, radio and all other kinds of media so that they may not be directly advertising for the product, but the images of people using and enjoying cigarettes as they go about their daily lives was never far from the view of global society. Some of the brainwashing tricks made popular through this kind of product campaign included little, but powerful, elements like making sure that the person holding the cigarette in the film or picture was always smiling and laughing or choosing the right colors and fonts to draw people in and make them want to go directly to the store to pick up a pack.

Layers Of Lies: The Steps For Successful Brainwashing

Individual techniques have no effective influence when it comes to trying to brainwash someone. Brainwashing is a process that involves a carefully chosen collection of techniques that are determined based on the target, the intent and the amount of time the agent has to achieve their ultimate goal or the brainwashing process. Regardless of the specifics, the basic layers of brainwashing are consistent for those who are learning about, practicing and perfecting their techniques.

1. **Rewrite The Past:** This first step is the most critical when it comes to successful brainwashing. Rewriting a person's past starts with making them question their beliefs, their history and anything else they have learned and hold dear. If the brainwashing agent is not able to make their target doubt what they know, then there is no way they will be able to implant new knowledge and beliefs (subliminally or forcefully). Once someone begins to doubt themselves, they become more open to new beliefs, searching for answers in their

unfamiliar surroundings and suddenly uncertain view of the world.

2. **Inspire Guilt:** Guilt is a powerful emotion that brainwashing agents take advantage of in order to further manipulate their targets into changing their thoughts, feelings and behavioral habits. By the end of the first stage, the target is rejecting everything they have ever thought or believed (assuming the brainwashing is going successfully) and they have been presented the new thoughts and ideas that their agents want them to embrace. While they may be reluctant to just start embracing new world views or changing their actions immediately, once they not only reject their past views, but feel guilty about them, they are more likely to become less confrontational and more cooperative for future thought and reality manipulation.

3. **The All Is Lost Moment:** This is a common occurrence for storytellers and writers who wish to create a moment of weakness for their protagonists to overcome. The "All Is Lost Moment" comes when a person is pushed to the point of hopelessness when it comes to factors like:

    -   Who they are, their personality and their view of the world

- Where they have been and what they have done to become the person they are now (the person that they are doubting and have lost all faith in)
- What they want for the future and how they see themselves getting there, if at all
  - A couple of the risks of brainwashing to the point of hopelessness is the high chance of suicide by the target or the chance of them hurting others after losing their value for human life

4. **Reaching Out & Making An Offer:** Brainwashing is a very lonely process for the target, even if they are part of a group thought manipulation. Once they have been psychologically worn down to the point of hopelessness (certainly by this stage in any successful brainwashing endeavor), it creates an opening for the agent to make an emotional connection, superficial or not, in order to gain their trust and make the final pull from their current psychological state to the agent's way of thinking or behaving.

   - The initial connection can be made with something as simple as bringing them a glass of fresh water, an extra portion of food or something else that they are wanting. This shows empathy (however feigned) toward the target and makes them more open to conversation or to taking action. A small act of kindness or human moment takes the agent from villain to potential ally to a desperate target ready to change their circumstances.

5. **Confession & The Compulsion To Get Involved:** Seeing a way out or a way to make things better makes people want to admit to embracing anything that will make them feel better and that they are making the right decision. By this phase, the target is fully under the agent's control with little chance of breaking free before the conclusion of the plan and the consequences that follow. They may still have hesitations, but they are far more open to persuasion and other brainwashing techniques if the process needs to be reinforced.

6. **Acceptance & Rebirth:** In this final phase, the target fully accepts the brainwashing process, embraces the new truths they have been fed and becomes the new person they have been designed to be through careful training, teaching, influencing and sometimes even physical torture (not technically a brainwashing technique, but often used in political, wartime, criminal and other darker uses of brainwashing to control prisoners, victims and captives).

Once all of these steps have been accomplished to their fullest (or their most effective depending on the circumstances) then the brainwashing process can be considered complete and the agent can take a look at the list of events that have taken place to see how successful they were in their endeavors. When it comes down to it, psychological studies have shown that brainwashing is one of the least successful methods of mental and emotional influence that people can invest their time in because it is so complex and the individual effects of all the different methods have yet to be fully studied. The main question that experts ask about brainwashing techniques and have been asking since the beginning is whether it is as powerful a manipulation tool as people think it is (worry or hope it is) because of the brainwashing process itself or because of the susceptibility of individual targets to psychological influence. From there they ask questions like what makes some people more susceptible than others and can be established brainwashing techniques be employed across genders, races and social classes to the same effect as others, or can certain factors and steps get lost in translation?

Common Brainwashing Techniques Used

In Both General & Dark Psychology

One brainwashing technique often seen in various industries and circumstances is the repetition of the fact or belief they want the target to embrace. This can be done through audible means like listening to a sound clip on repeat or through visual means such as forcing the target to write a phrase over and over until it is all they can think about or putting it a video clip that is then played on repeat as the only source of light or sound in the target's containment area.

Another technique involves getting a person to abandon their logical thought process and rely on their emotional impulses to determine their decisions, thoughts, and actions. Emotional impulses can be driven by a variety of factors such as defensiveness from fear of rejection or angry outbursts that happen because the target has been overwhelmed by the agent to the point of being so overwhelmed that they start to lash out at others instead of taking a deep breath and thinking before they do anything or accept any offers. One of the ways agents can do this is by taking the time to constantly distract their target by feeding them snippets of information (that may or may not be true) just to the point of getting them interested in that instead of what they have been distracted from and then keeping any further information on the subject to themselves. This withholding of information keeps the target coming to them in order to learn more to feel as if they are broadening their knowledge of the world. This makes them more open to influence when the agent feels ready to start the brainwashing process in its full strength.

Emotional control and manipulation are common techniques in brainwashing, mostly once the agent has already earned the trust of their target and is ready to start advancing their plan. This technique involves altering the emotional state of their target either by inducing fear or encouraging the recollection of painful memories until the target is so overwhelmed with emotion that they are unable to see that they are being influenced or even think that something wrong. Experienced brainwashing agents find a way to make their target feel comforted by their presence or at their willingness to sit and listen to their emotional issues, particularly if they are someone who does not easily expose themselves and their emotions to other people.

The Effects Of Brainwashing On

Individuals & Groups

The effects of brainwashing itself (and how effective it is a method of psychological control) have been called into question by different groups of researchers and experts who have spent years studying the American soldiers who returned to the United States after being released from the war camps, but were labeled as victims of brainwashing at the time of their return. They claimed that the ones they did speak to were most likely converted through the physical torture and neglect they underwent and not the actual brainwashing process. Their main reason for thinking this is that of the tens of thousands of prisoners put through brainwashing experiments, less than two dozen fell under the effects with any success. However, this total only takes into account the soldiers who decided to return to the United States, and not those who were so turned against the home country that they decided to remain in the land of their captors even after the war was over and everyone was released.

Cults around the world have played a large role in the continued interest of brainwashing and its effects. From the outside, it is easy to say that cults are bizarre and difficult to understand why anyone would want to get involved in one, but the brainwashing, manipulation and other influential practices of psychological control by the leaders or recruiters of these groups are some of the most practiced and well-tested agents and manipulators in human culture. The main way they accomplish this is by targeting people who are most open to influence, making them special and part of a community and then convincing them through fake friendship or understanding that what they are doing or standing for is genuinely right and good.

Successful brainwashing can have a number of effects on individuals and groups of people in the long run. Some of the most common side effects that can be eased or reversed through a process of un-brainwashing (more commonly known as *deprogramming*) include:

- Shattered sense of confidence
  - This can often lead to a series of painful and damaging decisions after the fact such as dependence on alcohol or the use of stronger drugs
- Inability to trust people
  - From every random encounter to those they love with all their heart, people who have survived the brainwashing process (successful or otherwise) tend to retreat into themselves, unsure of how to trust people they are surrounded by after their ordeal
- They see everything as a test
  - A lot of life loses its excitement after a brainwashing process. The victim rarely has any interest in events or activities they once enjoyed, they have lost their drive and enthusiasm for the future
  - Each time they are offered an opportunity or invited to join in on a task, they hesitate and make sure to pull apart and analyze every detail before even thinking about whether or not it is something they want to take part in

How To Protect Yourself From Becoming The Target Of Malevolent Brainwashing Techniques

Who is most susceptible to brainwashing techniques? Who is the most likely to become a victim of those seeking to improve their standing or just tear down others by convincing people to change their view of the world (sometimes a complete flip)?

One of the most common reasons people get drawn into cults or into the control of a manipulative agent is that they have no idea what brainwashing actually looks like or what kinds of warning signs to look for. The first way to protect yourself from falling prey to these types of psychological predators is to recognize the traits they look for in potential targets such as:

- Loners who have never found their place, but have no given up on finding where they belong or who they fit in with

- o This is one reason those runaway teenagers are often targeted by brainwashing cults and similar groups. They have not yet developed the emotional maturity or life experience to realize they are being taken advantage of in most cases.
- They do not have anyone to stand up for them
    - o This could be because they are anti-social by nature, but it is more likely because they are too stubborn to take the advice of others and have a tendency to get defensive when they are told what to do or that they should be more careful
- They are searching for answers or for a purpose
    - o This is when potential targets are drawn in by friends, family members, mentors or others that they know or have come to respect and trust. In cases like these, the agent uses their familiarity with the target and their knowledge of how they see the world in order to gain control of them
    - o Providing their target with a sense of duty to get them on board with the brainwashing process is the first step that is then followed by inspiring feelings of guilt and disappointment in the target when they have hesitations or fail at their assigned task

No one thinks they are susceptible to brainwashing. In fact, the concept itself conjures images of malnourished prisoners forced to watch propaganda videos until they accept them as truth and captured spies being injected with clear liquids that alter their mental state in order to change their reality by chemical means. However, brainwashing is not always as dramatic but can still be as harmful and dangerous. Once a person has determined whether or not they have the potential to become a victim, the next step is to look for warning signs that brainwashing is happening around you. Some of the most notable and widely established include:

- Unfamiliar, confusing and often increasing sense of fear connected to the world outside of their home or wherever they are currently living
- Constant feeling of inadequacy even when they know they have done their absolute best
- Feelings of mistrust and struggles with anxiety attacks over not impossible, but often improbable events like natural disasters striking out of nowhere, the fear of terrorist attacks at each place they visit from public restrooms in their local grocery store to the sidewalk corner across from their living quarters
- Abandonment of communication devices (no cell phone or social media allowed) and disconnect from people they are usually social with

All of these warning signs will be reinforced, promoted and even introduced if they do not develop on their own by the people doing the brainwashing. Any time you feel these feelings, particularly if you are experiencing multiple signs at once, look at the actions and behaviors of the people you consider your friends, your partners, and even your superiors. If they make the feelings worse through the things they do or say, or mock you for thinking something is wrong, then it is possible that they are running a brainwashing process on you. From here, the next step is the most difficult because it involves either denying what you are suspecting as just your imagination or that you are just going through a bad time, confronting the person about your suspicions (although this rarely leads to any kind of resolution, giving the agent in question only more opportunity to manipulate your emotions and feelings to whatever they want you to believe, most likely through guilt or through reminding you of your personal connection, or by removing yourself from the situation and severing ties permanently o until you have a better grip on your mental state).

Whether brushed off as fiction in favor of more solid mind control methods like physical pain and health neglecting or embraced as worrisome and complex method of psychological manipulation, brainwashing still has a lot to offer in terms of how the human mind works, how different people react in different situations and just how confident people can be in who they are and what they believe in. There is no limit of studying going on around the world and it is certain that experts on the subject have only just begun to peel away the layer of intricacy that is involved in the field.

Chapter 6: Handling The Hazards Of Hypnosis & Other Dark Psychology Methods At Use In Broad Daylight

Hypnosis has become a globally recognized and respected form of treatment for psychologists and counselors that have been trained in the art of hypnotizing patients. Not everyone can benefit from hypnosis therapy, but it is especially helpful with patients that have deeply suppressed memories or emotions that are knowingly or unknowingly affecting their behavior.

When people picture hypnosis, some of the images that appear include swinging pendulums and a quiet but consistent ticking noise that lulls people into a state of total relaxation. Once in this relaxed state, people are more open to sharing their thoughts and feelings which is great when hypnosis is used as a tool for promoting someone's mental health. There are also some dark uses for hypnosis though that are favored by those who are looking for more gentle and subtle methods of persuasion and manipulation than those who study Dark Psychology typically opt for.

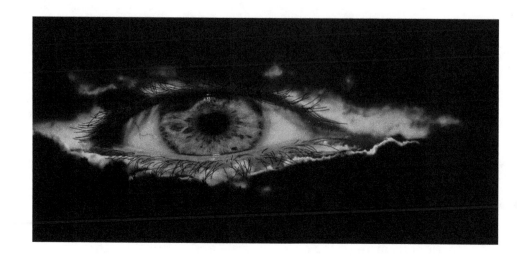

Dark Psychology Basics: What Is Hypnosis & How Does It Work?

Hypnosis may have many uses that can be wielded with various levels of success depending on a person's intent and ultimate goals for it as a psychological management tool. At its most basic level, hypnosis is defined as a cooperative action taken by a trained hypnotist and another individual with the intention of assisting that person with better understanding their own mental and emotional states.

Hypnotism has roots leading all the way back to pre-Christianity days in Persia, Greek, Central Europe, and the

Middle East when it was used as a method of meditation for some and studied as a valuable form of medicine by others. Kings of the time were believed to possess healing powers and would perform ritualistic hypnosis procedures and processes on their followers to cure ailments from headaches to nightmares and physical pains that were entirely psychological. Some have described it as a form of magical medicine while others take a more realistic approach and embrace it as a trance-like state that opens the mind in ways that humans cannot achieve by themselves. In their opinions, when the mind is open like this (through effective hypnosis and the guidance of a trained hypnotist), man can reach levels of personal understanding and understanding of universal laws beyond what is attainable when they are in their average daily mental and emotional state. Due to this belief, many experts in hypnosis have dedicated their lives and careers to the pursuit of further knowledge through hypnotism and meditation, trying to unlock hidden areas of the brain (for those who believe that humans only use a small portion of our mental capacity but have the ability to rise to our full potential through hypnotic techniques).

- FUN FACT: The study of hypnosis and some of the more mystical techniques and procedures were developed by a man named Franz Mesmer of Austria who was known for putting on a black wizard's cloak, playing soft, but strange music during his hypnosis sessions and using magnets in order to help connect people to their higher frame of mind. These mystical and ritualistic behaviors are a part of why many people think of magic and chants when they think about hypnotism instead of its benefits as a therapeutic tool. Franz Mesmer is also the inspiration behind the word "mesmerizing". To mesmerize someone means to completely draw and hold their attention or focus for a period of time. When someone or something is mesmerizing then he, she or it has the ability to capture someone's attention and concentration while also inspiring feelings of awe or ease. This word often goes right next to hypnosis in people's minds when the subject comes up.

There are tons of benefits that have been linked to hypnosis that has driven it to be used for a variety of purposes:

- Therapeutic hypnosis can be used in the treatment of physical pain reduction for people who are in recovery after an injury or suffering from a chronic disease
- It can also be used in the treatment of painful or crippling diseases that have no distinguishable medical cause but have been linked to psychological induction of symptoms and illness

- Hypnosis has been shown to assist with recovery from addictions such as alcoholism and dependency on harder drugs
- It can also be used to stop compulsive behaviors like shopping to the point of bankruptcy or anger management lapses that lead to emotional outbursts
- In the early 1800s, hypnosis was also reportedly used as a means of anesthesia before surgeries or when treating patients with painful symptoms

One of the most common misconceptions about hypnosis is that the individual being hypnotized is coming under the total mental control of their partner and giving up their ability to make decisions or control their actions. While the laid back mental state created through hypnosis techniques does make people more susceptible to persuasion and subliminal influence, the person doing the hypnotizing has no actual control over the person's actions. One of the reasons this is such a widely believed fact is that the use of hypnosis techniques has often been used as an excuse by people who have survived cults and terrorist groups. While there is little evidence that hypnosis actually has the ability to make people take actions they would not do on their own such as participate in a bank robbery or smuggle an explosive into a building, it is a popular excuse because it removes responsibility for the individual who is most likely struggled with accepting, acknowledging or explaining their behavior to a court or to their loved ones. The main purpose of a hypnotist is not to engage in mind control techniques once their subject is fully hypnotized, but rather to act as a guide through their detached and centralized state of psychological focus.

Pro Tip: Find A Professional, If Only To Learn From

There are thousands of different hypnosis techniques that someone can choose from to find the most effective tactics for handling their issues or reaching their personal or professional objectives. Put a quick search in online and there are dozens of pages of results that come up, each one claiming to have information on the best hypnosis methods, practices, and exercises for people wanting to learn more about the art. With so many options for how to approach hypnosis and so many people wanting to share their personal success with others, many people end up trying the first few they find and quitting when those first few methods do not work for their individual needs.

The best way to not give in to the crushing weight of all that knowledge is to take a more focused or localized approach. Unless you live in a very small town or a secluded area, research shows that most average American towns have at least three to five different therapists or psychologists available for consultations on any range of psychological concerns. In towns where there is a large psychological section in the medical community, people looking for information on psychological hypnosis methods and theories have a better chance of finding a specialist that has firsthand experience or licensed training in therapeutic hypnosis. For those who do not have a large selection of psychological experts to contact in their area, all licensed psychologists have spent some time studying therapeutic hypnosis in the pursuit of their degrees. Regardless of whether you are looking to be hypnotized as a form of therapy, whether you have questions about the darker side of psychological hypnosis or whether you just want to know more about the topic in general, a professional will be able to answer your questions and even make recommendations about next steps or where to seek practical experience opportunities. Even if you do not want to be hypnotized, someone who has studied the theories or practiced it themselves are the best source of knowledge and information that anyone interested in learning about Dark Psychology and hypnosis could ever ask for!

Hypnosis works by following a carefully laid out process that can be adjusted (if necessary) by those who have studied their chosen techniques and have experience handling potential challenges that arise with hypnotizing someone. It is important to keep in mind that not everyone is a good candidate for hypnosis techniques, in fact, less than 20% of the population responds to hypnosis as they would have hoped to go into their first session. The reason for this is because hypnosis is merely a means of making someone more open to influence. Anyone who has strong emotional, mental or psychological barriers is less likely to be successful as the subject of hypnosis while those who have little emotional maturity or experience to have shaped their psychology, such as children and those with mental conditions that affect their ability to control their thoughts and emotions, are more easily swayed into hypnotic states thanks to the welcoming and comfortable environment created each time a hypnosis session starts.

Different Types Of Hypnosis Techniques To Take Advantage Of Or Be On The Lookout For

The first step to any kind of hypnosis is to make certain that the target or the participant is someone that already believes that hypnosis really works. If the person being hypnotized is someone that thinks hypnosis is a joke or some kind of gag that people use for supernatural entertainment then there is no way that psychological hypnosis is going to be successful, if it has any effect at all on their mental and emotional center of being. Those who try to use hypnosis as a Dark Persuasion or Dark Manipulation tool will search for targets that already speak positively about hypnosis or people that may not fully believe in its abilities but also do not have any reason to doubt and want to believe that it works. Having the person being hypnotized believing that hypnosis is the answer for them is the hardest part of the battle.

Once this is achieved and the participant is ready or the target is chosen and primed, the next step if for the hypnotist to choose the right kind of hypnosis technique to meet their needs. In most cases, the determining factor for this is going to be intent, either on the part of the hypnotist or the participant. In this section, we are going to look at some examples of effective hypnosis techniques and how they work with human psychology.

Pro Tip: Consent Is The Legal & Ethical Way To Perform Hypnosis On Others

With many of the Dark Psychology methods and practices, they work best when the target does not realize they are being psychologically influenced by another person. Hypnosis does not work like this because, in order for it to be effective, the subject needs to actively participate in the hypnosis technique that has been chosen and agreed upon. For those who study and are looking to start practicing hypnosis, it is critical to always make sure to get consent before ever trying to hypnotize someone. Most experts would recommend getting it in writing or recorded so that if the subject takes any actions or makes any decisions that have negative consequences they later do not want to take responsibility for, they can claim that they did it under your influence after being unwillingly hypnotized (sometimes used alongside brainwashing in areas where consent is not necessary because there is no moral or ethical precedent set). This can cause a lot of legal trouble for those who practice hypnosis and similar psychological subconscious access methods because while there is no way to prove that they really were or were not acting under instructions given to them subliminally through hypnosis, lack of consent (and lack of proof of that consent from the hypnotist) are almost guaranteed to bring down legal troubles that no one wants to get involved in.

- The best advice is to draw up a legal consent form that all targets or participants have to read and sign before being able to undergo hypnosis of any kind. This protects both the hypnotist and the participant in the event that there are troubles or challenges during and after the process.

The Conversational Cooperation technique is the most popular technique in use in modern medical practices and throughout the world. Have you ever wondered where ideas come from when they seem to just randomly pop into your head? Thoughts and ideas are created in the subconscious and presented to the conscious mind after the conscious and unconscious minds have had a chance to communicate and contemplate. This is the power behind the Conversational

Cooperation technique. Basically, this method is driven by the human brain's ability to use their conscious, unconscious and subconscious minds simultaneously in order to access and engage the part of their brain that can make plans or come up with solutions to problems. The Conversational Cooperation technique is the technique that is most represented in the media:

- The participant or target is in a relaxed but stable position in an environment that has been designed to inspire feelings of total comfort and safety
- They have their eyes closed or are focused on a particular image that draws their conscious mind into thinking about nothing other than the image and the sound of the hypnotist's voice
- The words chosen by the hypnotist can be something similar to a mantra or can be nothing planned but rather a series of softly spoken responses to any words or actions taken by the participant as they slide deeper into hypnosis

While it is effective, this technique does little when employed on its own and works better as a starting technique or method of hypnotic induction to be followed by additional and more advanced hypnosis practices that have been chosen based on the subject's needs or desires.

Another popular hypnosis exercise is the act of retraining someone's brain and to alter the way they perceive a part of their life or a part of the world. This is typically done for the benefit of the participant but can be used by those who want to try hypnosis as a brainwashing or manipulation technique. Beginning with meditation to help focus the mind and tune out all other thoughts or feelings than just what the participant is being encouraged to think or feel through the hypnotist's voice. This technique is most recorded and researched as being used on expecting mothers who are worried about how painful childbirth is going to be but do not want to (or cannot) take chemical medicine to help ease the distress when the time comes and in the hours leading up to the actual birth. Through hypnosis and verbal suggestion, a trained hypnotist can help the expecting mother retrain her brain by changing the way she views childbirth.

- When most people think about a woman having a baby, they imagine the poor mother howling in pain and squeezing the hands of the people that are with her until they lose feeling in their fingers. Just holding this image, or whatever image someone conquers up in their imagination when they think about childbirth is enough to increase the amount of pain felt for the mother during the event itself
- Using hypnosis, a trained hypnotist (who preferably also has some medical background and experience

related to maternity) can help the mother clear her mind of that image and replace it with more peaceful settings like dream vacation spots or imagined images of herself laughing throughout labor instead of crying.

- While it does not help with actual pain management needed for the physical changes happening to the body during labor, they can help with controlling mentally projected or intensified pains that are connected with the mother's frame of mind during the process of childbirth

Dark Psychology & Human Nature: Other Techniques At Work All Around Us

Dark Psychology is one of the most accurate and truthful representations of human nature available for study, collection and development into practical skills. There are a lot of different techniques that can be studied and practiced for those who are interested in learning about and mastering Dark Psychology.

Those who like to use Dark Psychology and related tactics on others for their own benefit do so because they not only know how to but also get enjoyment from preying on people's good qualities. One technique that can be used for this purpose is the art of seduction, which can be for romantic or manipulative final goals. By targeting people's good opinions of themselves like their love of their personal style or their high opinion of their own reflection, those who use seduction as a weapon are able to earn peoples' trust (often through compliments and boosting their vanity) before getting them to come closer either emotionally or physically in order to get them to do or believe what they say. Sex can be a powerful and dangerous motivator for both the person using it as a manipulation technique and for the person being manipulated. One way to protect yourself from getting involved with seductive manipulators is to practice self-care at all times, regardless of the length of the relationship, because as soon as you stop thinking about and looking objectively (or as objectively as possible considering that relationships starting with seduction often build strong emotional ties or connections that can be used for both influence and control in the wrong hands).

Flattery can be a powerful and effective tool for those who rely on their knowledge of others, how their emotions form and project, and their specific personality types in order to manipulate their thoughts, opinions, and actions. It can be a tricky business though that takes a lot of practice to master for a number of reasons but using flattery to get what you want is a common practice among con artists to ambitious social climbers looking to make their way up the management chain at their company. This technique is particularly popular with people that also display narcissistic and vain qualities as these people enjoy watching how others react to their positive comments even though they know that there is no substance to them.

For those who are interested practicing flattery as a psychological influence technique, most people who have years of experience would recommend for beginners to start their training to do it with strangers like the person behind the register at the coffee shop or someone they bump into on the street that they have never seen before. They choose people who they are already expected to be friendly with due to the rules of polite society, but that they do not necessarily have to interact with again if they stumble or embarrass themselves during the course of honing their flattery skills.

- To avoid falling victim to flattery as a psychological manipulation tool it is important for individuals to try and remain objective when receiving compliments, particularly if they seem to be coming from nowhere or if they are coming from someone that the person is unfamiliar with
- This type of technique creates what is typically referred to as a vanity trap. Vanity traps are successful for those who have good people skills because the person doing the flattering first builds an environment of comfort and trust and then boosts their target's confidence with compliments or other positive statements. This technique preys on everyone's primal needs to be liked and to feel good about themselves by knowing that others think positively about them
- Since everyone struggles with being held back by and experiencing these emotions at some point in their lives, everyone is susceptible to being targeted for

vanity traps by those who have learned how to wield flattery as a psychological weapon of control and influence over others

What Is Reverse Psychology & How Does It Work?

Reverse Psychology is the act of encouraging someone into a particular thought or action by supporting a contradictory statement or belief. This contradiction serves as a means of motivation as the person the Reverse Psychology technique is being used on now feels they have something to prove or feels they need to succeed in order to return the contradiction to the person who initially delivered it. It is often used as a tool for comedic purposes as it can be a cause of misunderstandings for those who are not familiar or comfortable with the subtleties of language and tone.

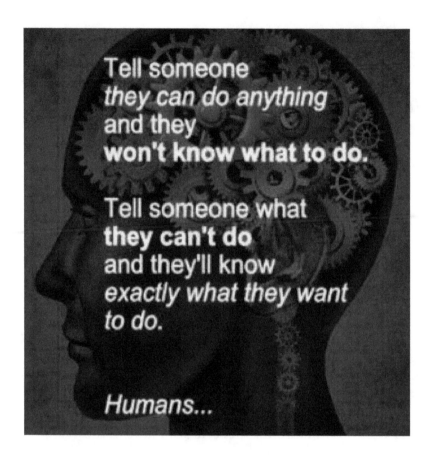

Tell someone
they can do anything
and they
won't know what to do.

Tell someone what
they can't do
and they'll know
*exactly what they want
to do.*

Humans...

The steps to mastering and effectively using Reverse psychology are simple and can best be explained through an example:

Someone spends most of their time criticizing and speaking down about the rise of electric cars. Despite their benefit to the environment, this person refuses to even get in one because they have such a bad opinion of them, preferring their large gas guzzling vehicle instead. When the time comes for them to get a new car, they find one that they like the look of and have read positive reviews of for months now. However, further research reveals that it is an electrically powered vehicle. Due to his negative view of electrical cars, he won't even consider taking it for a test drive and instead opts for another large gas guzzler that is more expensive on the monthly budget and slightly out of his price range.

His wife however likes the electrical vehicle he initially looked at but knows that he will refuse to even discuss it even though it will help to reduce their monthly expenses. Instead of taking the logical approach and reasoning with him, she decides to try Reverse Psychology so that he changes his mind about the electric vehicle and does so without ever questioning that it was completely his idea. Instead of telling him how much better it would be for them, she talks about all of the things that extra money could be going to and claiming that she doesn't mind going without. In this case, she is now using not only Reverse Psychology techniques but also other Dark Psychology techniques such as passive aggression (when she talks indirectly about going without because of all the money they spend on gas for the larger vehicles) and negative thought manipulation (when she starts to mention all of the bad aspects of the larger vehicles and following them up with remarks like, "But who cares about that?" in order to instill guilt and encourage him into action that makes her look more favorably on him and their situation.

No matter what your interest in Dark Psychology and the many different techniques, practices, and forms it can take, we hope you've enjoyed our guide and want to encourage everyone one to keep searching for information and never stop learning! That is how advancements and discoveries like the ones included in this book are found, formed, perfected and put to use in practical circumstances in all aspects of human life.

Conclusion

Thank you for taking the time to enjoy Dark Psychology: The Ultimate Beginner's Guide To Persuasion, Manipulation, Deception, Mind Control & How They Are Used To Influence People! Hopefully, you have finished the guide with eh better knowledge of Dark Psychology and the various sub-sections of study that have been established through years of study. The information contained in this instructive and enlightening guide was collected from the most educated and renowned sources so that our readers can be confident in their newly acquired knowledge.

We sincerely hope that you not only feel better informed about the dark side of human psychology and are prepared with the tools you need for developing your personal abilities in persuasion or other methods, but also that you are finishing our guide with the desire to know more and to never stop learning.

Now that you have a better grasp on what to do and how to do it, the next step is to actually put your newly discovered abilities into practice! If you read the guide to learn how to use Dark Psychology techniques to improve your personal or work relations and standing:

- Choose which techniques you want to try and lay out a plan of action that includes the method or methods you will need for success in accomplishing your goals
- Decide how many people you will need and where you can best find them (work, school, random acquaintances, home)
- Observe your target or targets and choose how best to make your initial approach

Pro Tip: Patience Is The Best Path To Success!

This is good advice for just about any kind of challenge or Dark Psychology and the techniques that make it such an effective tool for influencing people should never be rushed. The process can be frustrating (especially for those who are just getting started on developing their skills) but it is critical to remain calm, react to challenges rationally instead of impulsively, and always focus your energy on maintaining control of yourself, your target and the situation you have created.

If you are someone who was interested in *Dark Psychology: The Ultimate Beginner's Guide To Persuasion, Manipulation, Deception, Mind Control & How They Are Used To Influence People* to learn how to defend yourself from manipulative people or psychological predators:

- Work on your powers of observation and become a good listener
- Practice self-awareness and find a way to incorporate it into your daily routine
    - Reflect on the day when you get home each night or before bed, especially if you are feeling odd about a person or situation you encountered
    - Keep a diary so that you have a list of events, concerns and new connections that you make as you live your life so that you always have a record to look back on when you are feeling doubtful
    - Meditation is another good way of practice reflection and self-awareness that helps to center your thoughts and emotions so that you can see things more clearly
- Always ask questions when you are feeling concerned or curious about anything!
    - Learning to trust your instincts is a large part of this. While those who are experienced and well-practiced at psychological influencing may be able to do so without raising any kind of suspicion, if

you feel like something is wrong or if something is making you uncomfortable then there is probably a good reason for it

o   Asking questions makes manipulative people and other personality types that try to take advantage of people through psychological influence wary and helps to make you less of a target if there is a predator or Master Manipulator around you

Good luck with all of your future endeavors and don't forget to never stop learning! The more you are able to learn about each topic or opportunity that captures your attention, the more you will be able to use your knowledge of psychology, Dark Psychology and all of the different methods and techniques at work within them to boost your own standing and success!